"Being a missionary is intrinsic to being a disciple. However, from even a cursory survey of the standard thinking and practices in the church, one can be excused for thinking that this is not the case. In this fine book, Don brings missionality back where it rightfully belongs—in the basic, work-a-day spirituality of any authentic follower of Jesus."

ALAN HIRSCH, author of *Untamed* and *Right Here, Right Now*

"Get ready to dive in with your whole body and heart! With great humor and storytelling, Everts demonstrates that following Jesus is inextricably linked with going and doing God's mission in the world."

TOM LIN, vice president of missions and director of the Urbana Student Missions Conference, InterVarsity Christian Fellowship/USA

"Evangelical Christendom needs a book like this, which reframes its mission in a more accessible, more practical, more relational and more humane way. How I would celebrate if the missional believers approaching my friends in ghettos, in college dormitories, in gay bars, in Israeli and Palestinian villages, and in suburban neighborhoods all learned their moves from Don Everts. God would celebrate too, I think."

BART CAMPOLO, urban minister and activist

"This book reminds me of a doctor's physical (in a good way!)—skillfully checking under my tongue and knocking my knees to see if I'm spiritually healthy and sound. Then after the checkup, it offers me next steps to keep my soul in shape. Please read this book: it's a fresh, winsome and thoughtful articulation of what faith could look like in our seemingly normal lives."

JAMES CHOUNG, author of *True Story: A Christianity Worth Believing In* and *Real Life: A Christianity Worth Living Out*

"Don Everts has done it again. With sound biblical teaching and inspiring personal anecdotes, *Go and Do* calls readers to move beyond the 'safe, successful and happy' to a mature discipleship that actively pursues God's mission in the world."

ALEC HILL, president, InterVarsity Christian Fellowship/USA

"In the book *Go and Do*, Don Everts, with the wit, charm and way with words his readers have become accustomed to, helps us define a most important word. I am thankful for Don's model of blending theology, poetry and relationships. His writing helps us all as we attempt to bridge the chasm of good thoughts about loving others and the good deeds of making disciples. Thank you, Don!"

JOHN TETER, evangelism team leader, Evangelical Covenant Church, and senior pastor, Fountain of Life Covenant Church

"There is something growing in the hearts of Christians—something aching to bust out. Corresponding to this ache, many observers see something in the church that needs to burst into the public sphere. Don Everts rightly identifies this as a missional impulse. *Go and Do* shows us that *missional* is indeed not a word, but a life . . . and points us to such a life in doable, grace-based ways."

TODD HUNTER, Anglican bishop and author of *Giving Church Another Chance* and *Our Favorite Sins*

"For years, Don Everts has been communicating the simple, brilliant, world-changing good news of Jesus. Here's his latest masterpiece. May it inspire you, not only to believe something in your head but to do something daring with your life."

SHANE CLAIBORNE, author, activist and lover of Jesus

GOANDDO

Becoming a Missional Christian

DON EVERTS

IVP Books

An Imprint of InterVarsity Press
Downers Grove, Illinois

InterVarsity Press
P.O. Box 1400, Downers Grove, IL 60515-1426
World Wide Web: www.ivpress.com
E-mail: email@ivpress.com

InterVarsity Press® is the book-publishing division of InterVarsity Christian Fellowship/USA®, a movement of students and faculty active on campus at hundreds of universities, colleges and schools of nursing in the United States of America, and a member movement of the International Fellowship of Evangelical Students. For information about local and regional activities, write Public Relations Dept., InterVarsity Christian Fellowship/USA, 6400 Schroeder Rd., P.O. Box 7895, Madison, WI 53707-7895, or visit the IVCF website at <www.intervarsity.org>.

Scripture quotations, unless otherwise noted, are from The Holy Bible, English Standard Version, copyright © 2001 by Crossway Bibles, a division of Good News Publishers. Used by permission. All rights reserved.

While all stories in this book are true, some names and identifying information in this book have been changed to protect the privacy of the individuals involved.

Cover design: Cindy Kiple
Interior design: Beth Hagenberg
Images: old card: © Mike Bentley/iStockphoto
space rocket: © Tony Lyons/iStockphoto

ISBN 978-0-8308-3822-6

Printed in the United States of America ∞

green press INITIATIVE *InterVarsity Press is committed to protecting the environment and to the responsible use of natural resources. As a member of Green Press Initiative we use recycled paper whenever possible. To learn more about the Green Press Initiative, visit <www.greenpressinitiative.org>.*

Library of Congress Cataloging-in-Publication Data

Everts, Don, 1971-
 Go and do: becoming a missional Christian / Don Everts.
   p. cm.
 Includes bibliographical references.
 ISBN 978-0-8308-3822-6 (pbk. : alk. paper)
 1. Evangelistic work. 2. Missions—Theory. 3. Christian life. I.
Title.
 BV3790.E83 2012
 269'.2—dc23
                                          2012009655

| P | 18 | 17 | 16 | 15 | 14 | 13 | 12 | 11 | 10 | 9 | 8 | 7 | 6 | 5 | 4 | 3 | 2 | 1 |
| Y | 27 | 26 | 25 | 24 | 23 | 22 | 21 | 20 | 19 | 18 | 17 | 16 | 15 | 14 | 13 | 12 |

And Jesus said to him,
"You go, and do likewise."
LUKE 10:37

Dedicated to the memory of
Francesco di Bernardone
and
Agnes Gonxha

• • •

Contents

Introduction

Missional Is Not a Word

• • •

THERE IS SOMETHING incessantly, wonderfully bothersome about Jesus.

After a couple of decades of following him, I'd say this is perhaps what I love most about him. He's not content being my Savior, but also insists on being my Lord. He's not content with me knowing the right answers about the faith; he wants me to actually live by faith. He's not content with the ways I have been marked by God's work in this world (forgiven, healed, clothed, embraced); he seems equally interested in me getting caught up and involved in God's work in this world (as a witness, a neighbor, an agent of his kingdom).

Jesus has always been wonderfully bothersome in this way. Once a lawyer stood up to test him. This erudite man of words asked Jesus, "Who is my neighbor?"—not because he wanted to know the answer, but because the question was a handy rhetorical tool. Jesus responded with the parable of the good Samaritan, a timeless story that paints a radical picture of mercy, hospitality and love.

But Jesus wasn't content just telling the story. He wasn't interested in merely winning the debate or in having the lawyer shed a tear at the touching narrative. No, Jesus has always been more bothersome than that. So after telling the unforgettable story, he looked into the eyes of the lawyer and said, simply, "You go, and do likewise" (Luke 10:37).

Go and do likewise. Isn't there something wonderfully bothersome about those words? They don't leave you alone. They are like a firm, brotherly pat on the back, an urge to move forward, a daring invitation. This is definitely not where the calm lawyer saw things going. With these words Jesus swept the lawyer right out of the safe realm of the hypothetical and theoretical, and plopped him smack dab in the nitty-gritty land of real life. Jesus has always been, in this way, bothersome.

I think there's something refreshing and honest and real about the words "Go and do likewise." They are like a door flung open in the winter—ushering cold, brisk gospel air into the stuffy, warm house of cultural Christianity, where I am tempted to grow sluggish and sleepy. They wake me up. They remind me that Jesus isn't just my blessed Savior, but my insistent Lord. They point to the wonderful news that Jesus wants more for me than right answers and an elegant theology. He wants me to get caught up in God's work all around me. He wants me to be, in a word, *missional*.

A Missional Christian?

I feel the need to admit right from the get-go that there is something a bit odd about the word *missional* and the phrase *Missional Christian*. Even though more and more people are using *missional* these days, it's grammatically a bit of a stretch: we have plenty of nouns coming from *mission* (*missions, missionary, missiology*) and even some aggressive sounding verbs (*missionize, missioning*), but an adjective? *Mission-al?* Many dictionaries don't list such a word.

As if that weren't awkward enough, the phrase *Missional Christian* could also be accused of being unnecessarily redundant: being involved in God's mission on earth is part of what it means, at a basic level, to be a Christian. Clarifying that someone is a *missional* Christian is tantamount to saying that someone is a *Christian* Christian.

Awkward to say the least. This, I admit. And yet, grammatical awkwardness and theological redundancy aside, I have come to believe that *Missional Christian* is a necessary and important phrase.

If a Missional Christian is defined as a believer who is personally marked by and caught up in God's mission in this world, then indeed such a description *ought* to apply to every single member of God's church. But we have to be honest—this is not always the case. I know this from personal experience.

You see, when I became a Christian at the age of sixteen at a Young Life camp in Canada, my life changed indelibly. I was marked by God's work of salvation. The shock of forgiveness and the balm of healing were welcome new flavors in my life, and my posture toward God shifted dramatically during that week's mountain retreat. But, at first, my posture toward this world did not. Though I was *marked by* God's mission in this world (he came and saved me!) I was not *caught up in* that same mission. My posture toward the world around me remained much as it had before.

The Safe Christian

Growing up as a somewhat fearful introvert in a family that moved every few years, I had developed a very careful, very circumspect posture toward this world around me and the people who crowded near me. To be honest, that posture didn't change dramatically when I became a Christian.

I still carefully navigated my days, still avoided most people and still daydreamed about getting to live alone in a cabin in the woods someday. I was living life not as a Missional Christian but as a Safe Christian.

The Safe Christian looks around at this world and mostly sees threats. The Safe Christian is *marked by* God's mission in this world but is *caught up in* protecting himself from that world. Though I wouldn't have admitted it at the time, that's exactly what I was like. More than anything I wanted safety, space and healthy margins between this world and me. That's just the posture I had learned growing up.

Within my new faith I found a fair amount of justification for this posture: the world was full of temptations and sin and, well, *worldly* things. And as a Christian, I was to isolate myself from these negative influences. In this way I took the wonderful gospel call to holiness as a license to retain my fearful posture toward this world and thereby walked through many days as a Safe Christian.

The Successful Christian

Not everyone grows up with my temperament and fear, I realize. I've met many people whose primary drive in life isn't to hide from the world but, rather, to succeed in it. I've seen those same people discover Jesus and come to faith and change their entire posture toward God, only to have their posture toward this world remain unchanged. They become Successful Christians: believers who are *marked by* God's mission in this world but are *caught up in* succeeding in this world.

When Successful Christians look around them, they don't see a world full of danger (as the Safe Christian does) they see competition, people to compare themselves to and opportunities for advancement. Though they might not admit it, many Successful Christians aren't preoccupied with stiff-arming the world (as I was) but are instead preoccupied with climbing ladders, waving to get the attention of others and gathering as many trophies and accolades as they can.

Mind you, the pursuit of success can all be done in a very polite, Christian manner. We "give testimony" and share in public settings stories that allow us to brag about our own achievements or piety. We mask our love of money and stinginess under language about wanting to be "good stewards" of what God has given us. In this way we may try to baptize our worldly, ego-driven lust for success, but there's no hiding the fact that some Christians' posture toward the world is singly focused on succeeding.

The Happy Christian

We are very creative in how we interact with the world around us, and many of us just unknowingly, unthinkingly bring those same postures with us when we enter the kingdom of God. The Safe Christian and the Successful Christian have a posture toward this world that predates their life in Christ. The same is true of the Happy Christian.

The Happy Christian is *marked by* God's mission in this world but is *caught up in* enjoying the pleasures of this world. When the Happy Christian looks around at this world, she doesn't see dangers or competition; she sees a veritable amusement park. This world (especially for those with the means) is chock-full of rides and adventures and pleasures. There's food to try and countries to visit and malls to explore and favorite sports teams to watch and novels to devour and games to play and movies to watch and . . . The opportunities for someone with the means to tickle their own fancy are nearly endless.

In a world that profits from our entertainment and therefore artfully encourages our pursuit of it, the temptation to be a hedonist is rampant. In a consumer culture, it is almost assumed that our primary (though perhaps unspoken) posture toward the world around us is as consumers. This is the default posture many people have toward the world when they become Christians. And this posture can, sadly, go unchanged. For the Christian who is so inclined, there are plenty of Christian stores, Christian novels and Christian movies for them to enjoy. And at times our churches don't challenge this posture, but rather pander to it, treating us primarily as the entitled consumers we act like. At times it's enough to make a Christian think that a Happy Christian is the most normal kind of Christian in the world to be.

Becoming More Missional

This is where our potentially awkward phrase, *Missional Christian,* becomes so helpful. Every Christian is *marked by* God's mission in this world. But not every Christian is *caught up in* that same mission. Many of us are caught up in protecting ourselves from the world, succeeding in this world and enjoying the pleasures of this world. But there is another way.

Go and do likewise. Just as Jesus blew open the door of the lawyer's warm, stuffy, familiar house of words and theory, so he continues to this day to invite his followers to wake up from the slumber of their safety, success and hedonism, and breathe in the brisk air of his gospel call: go and do likewise. Jesus won't settle for us being *marked by* God's mission in this world; he is joyfully insistent that we get *caught up in* that same mission. As James S. Stewart pointed out, "To accept Christ is to enlist under a missionary banner."

Of course getting caught up in God's mission in this world is not something that happens all at once, but it is something that can and should happen to every Christian. Every Christian is called to partner with God in his work. No Christian is meant to be a bystander. And here's the really good news. Every Christian can become more missional over time. In fact, this is something Jesus is wonderfully insistent about. I know from personal experience.

As I said, I was primarily a Safe Christian when I returned from that Young Life Camp as a sixteen-year-old, brand-new Christian. I was changed by God, but still mostly reticent about his world around me. But then something began to happen: my posture toward this world began to shift slowly. Perhaps this change began from day one as a Christian, but I didn't notice it until months later when I found myself thinking about other students in my high school. I was accustomed to thinking about certain people in the halls of my high school (bullies to avoid; cute girls to, well, avoid), but I slowly began noticing other people as well (normal, sometimes hurting people).

These somewhat needy people represented neither threat nor thrill to me; they were people I never would have noticed before. But I found myself thinking about them and saying hi to them. Eventually (to my surprise) I found myself getting involved in their broken lives, motivated by a blossoming desire to serve and help them in some way.

This shift in my posture toward other high schoolers was but a small foretaste of a substantive shift in my posture toward this entire world. I have been slowly becoming less preoccupied with myself and more preoccupied with others. I am spending less time contemplating my plans and more time contemplating God's plans. Every year, I am getting more and more caught up in God's mission in this world. In a word, I am becoming more *missional*.

Don't Send Me to Africa

Becoming more missional has been a wonderful process, but I must admit I have spent a fair amount of time fighting against it. You see, this missional posture toward the world is a very particular posture—one that I was not accustomed to initially and one I didn't always see modeled or taught explicitly. And honestly, there was plenty inside me that wanted to just be a Safe Christian or a Successful Christian or a Happy Christian. And when I looked around me, I saw plenty of these species of Christians, enough to validate my varying desires to be safe, to be successful, to be happy.

It doesn't help that I have also spent most of my life rather allergic to the idea of being a missionary. Don't get me wrong; I have always admired missionaries from a distance, but they have always seemed to be such a very different species of Christian: rugged, strong, khaki-wearing adventurers who endure great physical deprivation (and a fair amount of social ridicule) for the sake of God's mission in this world. Missionaries, I've always figured, are like God's Special Forces.

And little old me? I've just never felt like Special Forces material. I feel very different from the exotic vocational Christian referred to with that sacred noun: missionary. That noun just puts the bar too high for me. And so I've been tempted, like many Christians are, to see mission as a thing for others. Mission is about them. Mission is over there. Mission is about them, there, then. Not me, here and now.

So I assumed. And yet, over time, an inexorable change has been taking place inside me. Month by month, Scripture passage by Scripture passage, risk by risk, one small decision at a time, I find myself getting more caught up in God's mission in this world. And it turns out, God's mission in this world is wider and deeper and, at once, more breathtaking and more humbling than I had ever imagined. As I journey on, I've met many others who are getting caught up in God's mission in this world too. This is a book about that journey.

Go and Do: Becoming a Missional Christian

But, in the end, is this a book about discipleship or about missions? That has been the most common question put to me during the writing of Go and Do. Am I writing about what it means to follow Jesus, or am I writing about what it looks like to engage in mission? The honest answer is: yes. In fact, the more I think about it, the more I find the presumed dichotomy between discipleship and missions to be, well, a little odd. And perhaps, in the end, that's what Go and Do is about.

This book is an attempt to reckon honestly with Jesus' joyful insistence that his followers are here on earth for a reason. It's also an attempt to relocate mission from the realm of the exotic and rare, squarely into the here and now. It is a survey of the core biblical truths about God's mission and God's people that other missional Christians have taught me. And it is, in the end, a celebration of how good God's mission is and what a tremendous miracle and gift it is that he allows us to be involved in it.

Part one, "Anatomy," is a description of the Christian who is getting caught up in God's mission in this world. A Missional Christian, it turns out, is different from a Safe or Successful or Happy Christian in some quite specific ways. This section is confessional and foundational and brutally honest. In particular, we'll be looking at the Missional Christian's eyes, hands, feet, heart and soul.

Part two, "Geography," is a survey of some of what God is up to in this world and how the average Christian can get caught up in this work. This section is very practical and mines the wisdom and counsel of Missional Christians who have gone before us. In particular we'll consider God's work in the family, among the lost, inside the church, in the city and around the world.

My two-and-a-half decades as a Christian, my fourteen years of working with college students with InterVarsity Christian Fellowship and my four years as a minister of outreach in a nearly two-hundred-year-old Presbyterian church in the suburbs of St. Louis have convinced me that *Missional Christian* (no matter how awkward or redundant a phrase it may be) is a necessary and important phrase. I pray that this phrase (as well as this book) helps us all get more caught up in God's exquisite mission in this world, going and doing all that God has for us.

PART ONE

Anatomy

What does Jesus tell us about
God's mission in this world
and our role in that mission?

And what will we begin to look like
if we get caught up in that mission?

1

Sober Eyes

Blessed are those who mourn.

MATTHEW 5:4

● ● ●

ALL CHRISTIANS PERCEIVE the world around them in some way. In that sense we all have "eyes." But that doesn't mean every Christian sees the world in exactly the same way.

The Safe Christian, I happen to know from experience, looks at the world with Fearful Eyes. Through these Fearful Eyes they look around at the world and see threats, risks and potentially dangerous variables. The Successful Christian, by contrast, tends to look at the world through Eager Eyes, seeing everything in a hierarchy and knowing precisely how they themselves stack up against others. Their Eager Eyes are always looking for a boost up, an advantage, collateral, a way to climb. And Happy Christians? They tend to glance around through slightly glazed Recreational Eyes. They see the world around them as if through rose-colored glasses, and what they see is mostly benign and often a potential way of enjoying themselves.

But what about Missional Christians? What kind of eyes do they have? It turns out that as Christians get caught up in God's work in this world, they begin to see this world quite differently. They begin to see the world as Jesus sees it, with Sober Eyes.

Jesus gave his disciples a clear idea of how he sees this world while sitting with them atop a hill one day, when he said,

> You are the salt of the earth, but if salt has lost its taste, how shall its saltiness be restored? It is no longer good for anything except to be thrown out and trampled under people's feet. You are the light of the world. A city set on a hill cannot be hidden. Nor do people light a lamp and put it under a basket, but on a stand, and it gives light to all in the house. In the same way, let your light shine before others, so that they may see your good works and give glory to your Father who is in heaven. (Matthew 5:13-16)

Jesus' words here are clear, brief and unambiguous. They teach us a lot about how Jesus saw the world, and how he saw his followers; namely, he saw this world as desperately needy, and his followers as uniquely designed to go with God into that world.

Salt of the Earth

"You are the salt of the earth," he said. Now, I personally use salt (sodium chloride) all the time to flavor my food. But I know a handful of sodium chloride felt different back when Jesus first spoke these words. In his day, salt was used primarily as a powerful preservative. In a world without refrigerators, freezers or crispers, meat quickly spoiled, becoming unhealthy and terribly odorous. Every single ounce of savory, protein-rich meat, once slaughtered, began to decay, to break down, to spoil. So holding a handful of blessed salt was like holding a fridge in your hand.

Salt was powerful because it did something to meat. Rub salt on decaying meat and you slowed down the decay. You arrested its inexorable downhill slide. In Jesus' day, they preserved meat with salt.

In Jesus' world, salt had a purpose. And standing with both feet in that world, he looked around at his followers and said, "You are the salt of the earth." His words echo across the centuries and whisper into every Christian's ears. They settle into the soul with weight: You are the salt of the earth. You have a purpose here on earth.

This is how Jesus saw this world, and his followers' place in this world. And Missional Christians begin to see this world and themselves in the same way. They see themselves as having a part in God's mission here on this decaying earth. They understand how odd it would be for them to never ever make contact with the decaying world around them. They take to heart Jesus' warning that salt that has lost its saltiness is good for nothing, that a Christian who isn't slowing the decay around him makes very little sense.

Light of the World

The Christian is also in this world as a light in the darkness. As Jesus put it simply, "You are the light of the world." In a world without streetlights, in a Capernaum that had never seen a light bulb, Jesus knew about darkness—deep, disorienting, confusing darkness. He knew the hopelessness that accompanied a broken lamp, the helplessness that accompanied running out of fuel for your lamp.

Darkness meant disorientation, missteps, mistakes. Darkness could mean cracked shins and wrong turns and misplaced treasures. Darkness could mean running your face into unseen (but very hard) walls. It could mean confusion. Jesus knew about darkness, which meant he knew about the true value of a lamp.

So it meant something quite specific and meaningful when Jesus claimed that he was "the light of the world." Jesus claimed to bring noonday clarity into this world. That which was hidden, obscured or confused in the darkness of the world became clarified by Jesus and his gospel. The light of Jesus brought clarity into the world. We see exactly which walls we've been running our faces into.

This same Jesus who came to enlighten the world then looked his followers in the eyes and said, "You are the light of the world." He saw his followers like lamps: little agents of Jesus' clarity, honesty and truth, helping blow the misleading mists of this world away, showing people what is true and clear.

Missional Christians understand themselves in this same way—as lamps intended to illuminate, to be used and displayed in dark places. The Missional Christian knows that no one in his right mind would ever put a lamp under a basket, as Jesus put it. Lamps are meant for stands. They are meant to be brought right into the darkest of places to bring clarity.

In short, the Missional Christian sees herself as having a purpose in this world. She sees herself as the salt of the earth, as the light of the world. In this way, Missional Christians have a hopeful, purposeful understanding of their lives. Their outlook on the world is imbued with hope: that which is decaying can be preserved, and the darkness can be displaced by clarifying light. And hope, it turns out, is a fabulous thing.

But there's a reason I have titled this chapter "Sober Eyes." If we are the salt of the earth and the light of the world, this means implicitly that the earth is decaying and that the world is darkened. Jesus was unambiguous on this point. He had Sober Eyes that saw the true need all around him, no matter where he was standing.

For example, when Jesus stood looking out over Jerusalem, he didn't marvel at the large city spread out before him. Instead he sighed a deep lament. When the leaders of the day engaged Jesus in conversation, he didn't eagerly seize the opportunity to climb social ladders. Instead he soberly used the moment to say, "Woe to you!" When a Pharisee invited him for dinner, Jesus didn't make endearing comments about the wonderful smells emanating from the kitchen. Instead he lamented the rancid smells of jealousy, pride and prejudice coming from the hearts of guests and host alike.

Jesus had Sober Eyes. He saw around him a world in need, a place of darkness and decay.

Living with Two Sober Eyes

No wonder, then, that Jesus would also say, "Blessed are those who mourn" (Matthew 5:4). I used to think he was kindly declaring a blessing over those unfortunate ones who were mourning. I now wonder if instead he was honestly declaring blessing over those who are not deceived into believing all is well in this world. Blessed are those who don't buy the smiley-face cover story. Blessed are those who don't ignore what is going on all around them. Blessed are those who see what's really going on, whose eyes are open. Blessed are those with Sober Eyes.

Not every Christian is so blessed. Safe Christians, after all, look around at this world with Fearful Eyes and see only threats to their safety. Successful Christians look around with Eager Eyes and see mostly opportunities for advancement, potential pedestals for their feet. Happy Christians see simply a benign world full of titillating options with their Recreational Eyes. The Missional Christian, in contrast, sees need.

Whatever room the Missional Christian walks into, she sees need—not potential danger to avoid, not a potential audience for her to perform for, not even potential amusements for her to get in line for, but a precious world that is dark and decaying. She sees a world that could use a little salt and light. In the parable of the good Samaritan, Jesus tells us explicitly that the priest, the Levite and the Samaritan all "saw" the man left for dead on the side of the road. But where the priest and Levite's Fearful Eyes saw only potential danger, the Samaritan's Sober Eyes saw a man in need.

After becoming a Christian, I slowly began to see the halls of my high school through Sober Eyes. I began to see need around me. In particular, I began to see need in two students, Christina and Dean. When I first met Christina and Dean, I didn't give either of them a second thought. They didn't represent a threat to me, and so in my posture as a Safe Christian, I turned my Fearful Eyes elsewhere in the halls of my high school. But the more I followed Jesus and the longer the Holy Spirit worked within me, the more I began to notice these two other students. I began to see them with Sober Eyes.

Christina was on the speech team with me, and I had always thought of her as a nice enough girl. But after becoming a Christian, I began noticing how heavy her spirit seemed. I felt a burden of sorts when I was around her, and I began mentioning Christina in my prayers to God.

The more I prayed, the more I began to wonder about the source of her heaviness. One Friday night, when some members of the speech team were going out to eat, I happened to be in the car that stopped by Christina's house to pick her up. And I met her dad. He was loud and abrasive, and drinking. I knew then where the heaviness was coming from. Behind Christina's thin smile was the undeniable presence of darkness and decay. She was walking under the load of a difficult home life, a dark secret that no one knew.

After seeing this, I was bothered. I used to see a nice girl, someone who was not a threat to me. But now I began to see darkness and decay, and a hurting girl who could use a little light and salt. God was beginning to give me eyes like Jesus'.

I began seeing Dean differently too. He mostly went unnoticed by our entire school. Thin and quiet, he walked through the halls slightly hunched over, seemingly glad not to be noticed, not to be the butt of anyone's jokes for a day. Dean's pain was evident enough, but I had never stopped to consider him as a person. (To be honest, I had always taken a measure of comfort from Dean's pain: as a new kid in the school who was painfully shy myself, Dean was proof that at least I wasn't at the bottom of the high-school food chain!)

But this changed when I became a Christian. I found myself noticing his hunched shoulders in the halls. And the longer I followed Jesus, the more I began to be bothered by Dean's pain.

As a brand-new Christian, I was learning to see the world—and myself—just as Jesus did. As Jesus said so clearly, "You are the light of the world. You are the salt of the earth." I began to realize that I was on earth for a purpose. I had been saved, I began to realize, into a life of purpose, of partnering with God in his work in this hurting world.

Blessed to Be a Blessing

Of course there was nothing new or novel about what was happening to me. God has always called his people to join him in his work. God called Adam to work the garden. And once the dreadful Fall occurred, he called people to partner in his grand mission of redemption. By calling Abram, God began to form a chosen nation so that they could partner with him in blessing the world. This purpose was crystal clear in God's initial call to Abram:

> Go from your country and your kindred and your father's house to the land that I will show you. And I will make of you a great nation, and I will bless you and make your name great, *so that you will be a blessing.* I will bless those who bless you, and him who dishonors you I will curse, and *in you all the families of the earth shall be blessed.* (Genesis 12:1-3, emphasis added)

Blessed to be a blessing. Saved to be salt and light. This is the cadence Abram experienced; it's the cadence Jesus' first disciples experienced. And, in the end, it's what every Christian is meant to experience. Every single Christian is blessed to be a blessing. We are marked by God's work in the world so that we can get caught up in that same work.

This is what I began to experience in high school. I already knew I was blessed, but God began to show me that I was blessed so that I could be a blessing. This was something of a startling revelation. If even shy, introverted, awkward me could be used as salt and light, then I knew God could use *anyone*. And, indeed, I have had the privilege of watching countless others get joyfully caught up in God's work in the world over the years.

Hans was a college freshman when I met him. I am something of an expert in introversion, and I can tell you that Hans was one of the most painfully introverted people I have ever met. One day when I came to campus to help him and his roommates bunk their dorm beds, I thought Hans wasn't in his room. The door was open, his roommates were there, but there was no Hans. I found out, though, that he was sitting in his closet. He had pulled a chair into his closet, and it turned out that he spent a fair amount of time in there. Now this was an introverted young man!

Could this young Christian ever be used by God as salt and light? Indeed. It began with a prayer time. A few of us were praying together in another dorm room, and Hans, normally so quiet and staid, began praying for the lost in North Korea. He prayed with such passion and detail—and volume—that I wondered what had gotten into him. Well, apparently Jesus had. Having grown up in Japan and South Korea, Hans had Sober Eyes to see the darkness and decay in North Korea, and that did something to him. And over time he began to see more and more of the world through those Sober Eyes.

In fact, Hans even began to see the students all around him through Sober Eyes. He no longer saw himself surrounded by aggressive students and parties and dangers that he needed to hide from in his closet, but rather he saw real people in need of salt and light. Hans got caught up in God's work on campus, eventually leading various Bible studies, reaching out in dorms and knocking on doors of complete strangers! Hans knew he was blessed to be a blessing and that changed how he saw the people around him.

Sometimes Christians, like Hans and I, need God's patient work in our lives to help our posture toward this world become more missional. Others seem to understand implicitly that they are blessed to be a blessing. Cypress has been coming to my church here in St. Louis for about a year now and recently gave her life to Jesus. A week afterward she asked about getting baptized. And a week after that (only two weeks after becoming a Christian) she joyfully signed up to volunteer at a center for homeless pregnant women that our church partners with in the city. Cypress was marked by God's work in this world and quite quickly is getting caught up in that same work.

It turns out this is a natural part of becoming a Christian. It always has been and always will be. And it often begins with the eyes. Before Christ, the world looked a certain way to us; after becoming his people, we begin to see the world differently. This was the case for one of my spiritual heroes, St. Francis of Assisi. Born Giovanni Francesco di Bernardone into a wealthy family, he saw the world around him through Recreational Eyes. He lived the unexamined life of an entitled youth, enjoying all the entertainments available to someone of his wealthy class. He lived the life of a playboy, seeing only fun and friends all around him.

But all this changed after he charged off to war in 1204 and was imprisoned. There God moved in his life, and Francesco had a deep conversion experience. Afterward, while recovering in Assisi, he began to see his hometown with new eyes, with Sober Eyes. He saw the neglected poor for the first time, and he saw the spiritual poverty and depression of the wealthy. This sobered view of the world around him led him to get caught up in God's work in that world—starting right there in Assisi.

Dwelling in a Land of Deep Darkness
I realize that, in a way, these are pretty drastic stories of darkness and decay: Christina's rough home life, the oppressive situation in

North Korea, homeless pregnant women and the depravities of thirteenth-century Europe. But are these exceptions? It can be tempting to view such cases as exceptions and conclude that *parts of the world* are indeed dark and decaying, but not the whole world!

But Jesus suggested that "the earth" is decaying and "the world" is dark. He had Sober Eyes that saw need all around him, whether he was looking at an old bleeding woman or a proud, wealthy man. Let's face it, his is a bracing, somewhat bothersome view to have of our world. Looking around with Sober Eyes is uncomfortable and disturbing. As a result, many of us resist such a view of the world. *Is it all really so bad?* we wonder. The answer from Scripture, as we follow the clear storyline from Genesis to Revelation, is yes.

Right after the Fall (Genesis 3), this beautiful, elegant, very good creation begins to unravel. It takes only a couple of chapters of decay for God to shake his head in lament: "The LORD saw that the wickedness of man was great in the earth, and that every intention of the thoughts of his heart was only evil continually. And the LORD was sorry that he had made man on the earth, and it grieved him to his heart" (Genesis 6:5-6).

Such an unqualified statement about God's reaction to the Fall should disabuse us forever of a lite view of the Fall and its consequences. Follow the storyline, and the unraveling, the decay, the darkening only continues, affecting every area of life. Even as God is knee-deep in his hopeful, messy mission of redemption, the darkness and decay are unavoidable. Isaiah cried along with all the prophets, "All we like sheep have gone astray; we have turned—every one—to his own way" (Isaiah 53:6).

Centuries later Paul would hand the Christians in Rome a sobering Old Testament description of the darkness and decay, using six quotes from the Psalms, Proverbs and Isaiah:

> None is righteous, no, not one; no one understands; no one seeks for God. All have turned aside; together they have

become worthless; no one does good, not even one. Their throat is an open grave; they use their tongues to deceive. The venom of asps is under their lips. Their mouth is full of curses and bitterness. Their feet are swift to shed blood; in their paths are ruin and misery, and the way of peace they have not known. There is no fear of God before their eyes. (Romans 3:10-18)

Because there is darkness and decay, God is on a mission of preservation and illumination, which is exactly why he sent Jesus. Remember that Isaiah didn't just lament the great need in this world; he also looked forward to the day when help would arrive: "The people who walked in darkness have seen a great light; those who dwelt in a land of deep darkness, on them has light shined" (Isaiah 9:2). John the evangelist described Jesus this way: "In him was life, and that life was the light of all people. The light shines in the darkness, and the darkness has not overcome it" (John 1:4-5 TNIV).

Jesus was unambiguous on this matter: "I am the light of the world. Whoever follows me will not walk in darkness, but will have the light of life" (John 8:12). And a little later, "The one who walks in the darkness does not know where he is going" (12:35). In other words, a world without Jesus wanders in darkened confusion.

There's just no way around this comprehensive view from Scripture. Paul wrote a letter to Christians to remind them, in the starkest of terms, of what their lives were like before Jesus:

And you were dead in the trespasses and sins in which you once walked, following the course of this world, following the prince of the power of the air, the spirit that is now at work in the sons of disobedience—among whom we all once lived in the passions of our flesh, carrying out the desires of the body and the mind, and were by nature children of wrath, like the rest of mankind. (Ephesians 2:1-3)

In short, they were like dead people walking around—like zombies. Paul gave a pretty sober view of life without Jesus and an apt illustration of what the Bible spells out cover to cover: the world is dark and decaying. And the same is still true today. We are still standing in a needy world.

Christians in a Land of Deep Darkness

God invites his people to live with eyes wide open. All followers of Jesus are invited to develop Sober Eyes, bravely admitting that we stand in a world that is dark and decaying. And this doesn't just mean the oppressed in North Korea or the displaced in turbulent Africa. Through Sober Eyes we see that there is need all around us.

Sometimes this need is obvious and hard to miss: wars are fought, food is hoarded, marriages crumble. The poor, the new, the different, the immigrant, the untouchable, the sick, the imprisoned and the elderly fester unseen. Suffer unseen. Sigh unseen. Handmade land mines unmake thousands, and mosquitoes kill millions for lack of simple, handmade nets. Sometimes the needs are obvious.

But sometimes the needs are more subtle, though just as real: curses fly from racist tongues, and blessings are swallowed in cynical throats; children are called names on the playground, and the elderly fade into insignificance in care facilities; boyfriends grow impatient, and girlfriends grow ashamed. The dust of boredom and fatigue and hopelessness begins to settle into the cracks of the human soul, and the machinations of human society rust and fall apart.

I've found that even the most seemingly benign, well-manicured landscapes are rife with need. Even those who live enwrapped in the seemingly safe, successful, happy accoutrements of suburban life, when they begin to look around their neighborhoods, their schools, their offices with Sober Eyes, begin to see the darkness and decay that Jesus spoke of, the walking dead that

Paul wrote of. There's darkness and decay all around us; it's as local as a child's heart, but its reach is global and systemic.

Practicing Praying the Psalms

When I first started looking around with Sober Eyes, I found it to be painful, shocking and even overwhelming. Sometimes it seems that there's just too much need and brokenness and it can be tempting to just close our eyes and pretend everything's okay. But rather than close or avert our eyes, Missional Christians need to relearn how to pray. I found that the calm, polite prayers I was accustomed to praying are simply inadequate when I begin to see the need all around me.

This is where the Psalms are so helpful. Eugene Peterson is right to call the Psalms "answering speech," because they help give us language for our prayers—even those angry, confused prayers that well up within us while standing amid the hurt and confusion of this world. I used to think the Psalms were flowery and joyful, and therefore pretty irrelevant. I couldn't have been further from the truth. Many of the psalms are yelling, angry, "I'm confused!" psalms. The cadence and language of the Psalms is a mighty help when first seeing the pains all around us. For those who are interested in learning from the Psalms, I suggest reading James W. Sire's very helpful book on this practice called *Learning to Pray Through the Psalms*.

Becoming More Missional

My own view of the world began to change as I walked along the halls of my high school. I was slowly becoming a Missional Christian with Sober Eyes, seeing the real world around me as

Jesus saw it. Since then, Jesus has continued to shape and alter how I see this world. My eyes become a bit more open, a bit more clear every year I follow him, seeing more and more the pains that people carry around with them, the dysfunctions in our families, the tensions that fill our cities—the darkness and decay that has spread to every square inch of this world.

But even as a brand-new Christian, I began to sense the place of a Christian in the midst of such hurt. I felt the burden that comes with a clear vision of the need all around—and I realized I had to do something about it.

You see, it turns out Missional Christians don't just look around with Sober Eyes; they begin to reach out, in practical ways, with Servant Hands.

2

Servant Hands

Whoever would be great among you must be your servant.

MARK 10:43

● ● ●

MOST CHRISTIANS have very busy hands. We work, do chores, comb our hair, play guitar, cook food, fix cars—our hands are almost constantly in motion. But while our hands may be occupied with a wide variety of activities from day to day (from the banal to the risky to the ordinary), I think they tend to be preoccupied with an overarching task.

Safe Christians, for example, tend to use their Defensive Hands to stiff-arm the world around them and protect themselves. Successful Christians' Grabby Hands are often busy gathering toward themselves accolades and trophies and compliments, while Happy Christians' Giddy Hands are preoccupied trying to find the latest recreational, social pleasure. We occupy our days with what preoccupies us in life.

Jesus had very specific thoughts about what his followers ought to do with their hands, and he gave his closest disciples an unforgettable image of this while sitting with them in an Upper Room in the middle of Jerusalem:

When he had washed their feet and put on his outer garments and resumed his place, he said to them, "Do you understand what I have done to you? You call me Teacher and
Lord, and you are right, for so I am. If I then, your Lord and
Teacher, have washed your feet, you also ought to wash one
another's feet. For I have given you an example, that you also
should do just as I have done to you." (John 13:12-15)

Washing Dirty Feet

When I read the Upper Room discourse in John, my Sober Eyes
are transfixed by Jesus' two hands as he dips the servant's rag into
the wash basin, as he takes his disciples' dirty feet in hand and
washes them. His two hands serve in humility. They are the rough,
humble hands of a servant.

In Jesus' day, this dirty job of washing people's feet was for servants. Low-ranking servants, in fact. It was a needed task, because
the traveler's feet grew dusty and sweaty with the rigors of travel
on dirt roads. For a guest to arrive and have his feet washed before
reclining at a meal was a great kindness. But to wash another's
feet? This was an onerous and dirty thing to put your hands to.
Notice that at the Last Supper not a single disciple was willing to
wash his own feet before the meal.

And we're told that, during the meal,

Jesus, knowing that the Father had given all things into his
hands, and that he had come from God and was going back
to God, rose from supper. He laid aside his outer garments,
and taking a towel, tied it around his waist. Then he poured
water into a basin and began to wash the disciples' feet and
to wipe them with the towel that was wrapped around him.
(John 13:3-5)

In spite of his divine origin, in spite of the authority God had
placed into his two hands, Jesus used those hands in the humble

task of a lowly servant. So dizzying and paradigm-breaking was it to see Jesus washing feet that Peter begged Jesus not to wash his own. Yet Jesus needed to give his disciples an unforgettable illustration of what he and his followers were to do with their hands: serve others.

Jesus was quite explicit on this point. Once, when his disciples were bickering over how they stacked up against one another, Jesus told them that his followers were to live quite differently from the world in this regard:

> You know that those who are considered rulers of the Gentiles lord it over them, and their great ones exercise authority over them. But it shall not be so among you. But whoever would be great among you must be your servant, and whoever would be first among you must be slave of all. For even the Son of Man came not to be served but to serve, and to give his life as a ransom for many. (Mark 10:42-45)

Greatness is found in servanthood, Jesus said. At every turn he modeled this and made it clear his disciples were to follow suit. "I have given you an example," he said after slowly washing each disciple's dirty feet. "If I then, your Lord and Teacher, have washed your feet, you also ought to wash one another's feet. For I have given you an example, that you also should do just as I have done to you" (John 13:14-15). Here it becomes unavoidably clear what Jesus' followers are to do with their two hands while on this earth: serve. Find dirty feet and wash them. What do Christians do with their hands in this dark and decaying world? They put them to use.

The Form of a Servant

The call to serve is for every Christian. "I have given you an example," Jesus said. The clarity and simplicity of the example wasn't lost on Paul, who wrote, "Have this mind among yourselves, which is yours in Christ Jesus, who, though he was in the form of God, did not count equality with God a thing to be grasped, but made himself nothing, taking the form of a servant, being born in the likeness of men" (Philippians 2:5-7). Every Christian, Paul wrote, is to have this same servant mindset.

And Paul got very specific about what it means to live with the posture of a servant. "Do nothing from rivalry or conceit, but in humility count others more significant than yourselves. Let each of you look not only to his own interests, but also to the interests of others" (Philippians 2:3-4). He couldn't have put it more plainly. Look to the interests of others—just like a servant would.

A servant's job is to defer, to look to others' interests. Servants understand that they are in the room to serve others, so they don't hesitate to anticipate needs and fill them. They grab up the rag and wash basin, and wash dirty feet. Taking the form of a servant is simple, really. Painfully hard and costly, but simple. At one point Jesus summed up servanthood: "And as you wish that others would do to you, do so to them" (Luke 6:31). In this way Jesus invites us to allow our well-developed "self-interest muscles" to guide our service. We know exactly how we want to be served and cared for, so it's often perfectly clear to us how we could serve others. As you wish that others would do to you . . . In this we have great guidance for service.

For example, if I were carrying two large suitcases, I know what I'd want done for me. (*Boy, I wish someone would come take one of these!*) So I take your suitcase for you—the heaviest suitcase—because I'd want someone to take the *heavier* one from me. And I insist. And I carry it the whole way—again, because that's what I'd want done for me. In this way our selfish instincts are wonderful guides to how to serve the needs of others around us.

Another example: if I were a lonely person but finally got up the nerve to try a new group at the nearby church, I would want someone to come up to me, ask me questions, show an interest in who I am. So, as a servant, when I show up to a meeting, I don't just look around for my friends. I also look around for new people to greet.

If I were slowed down by age, seated by illness or dulled by medicine, I'm sure I would want someone to stop and notice me—and not just say a few kind words and rush off, but take time to sit, unhurried, with me. So, as a servant, I remember those who are sidelined in life; I make time to slow down and sit with them. I sit with them and hold their hand, and smile.

If I were about to make a terrible mistake, I would want someone to say something to me. So, if my friend is about to make a terrible mistake, I tap her on the shoulder and shake my head. As a servant, I try to speak truth in grace.

"As you wish that others would do to you" is a clarifying guide for our service, no matter what the context: work (if your working group is fatigued and needs someone to muscle up the energy to lead, as a servant you lead); parenting (if it's been a hard day at school for your son, if he wasn't included in the games at recess, as a servant you close the laptop and talk with him about it, and maybe you even play kickball after dinner); marriage (if the baby starts crying again and you pretended to sleep through the last feeding—you slip out of bed quietly and do your part).

Service is often quite simple: every last disciple in that Upper Room knew that all the feet in the room were filthy dirty. But it was Jesus who got up, put the towel on and took the form of a servant. This act of washing dirty feet is what the Missional Christian is called to do with her two hands while here on earth. When the Christian gets up in the morning she doesn't just busy herself tending to her own interests. She looks around the room, around the house, around the world—and tends to others' interests also.

My friend Mike has been a great model of this for me. When we lived together, Mike was always anticipating my needs, going out of his way to help me or one of our friends who was over at our place. I don't think I ever saw Mike get up from the couch in our living room without checking to see if he could get something for someone else. Often he wouldn't ask; he was able to anticipate what the people around him needed and just brought it without even being asked. It was humbling to live with someone who took such joy in putting others' needs ahead of his own.

Cindy, a friend of mine at church, also has Servant Hands. Wherever I am at our church, I seem to run into her serving others. Whether she's leading a meeting, helping stack chairs, preparing food for someone else's meeting, writing a thank-you note or washing dishes—whatever room Cindy's in, she is looking for ways to serve. While riding the Moscow subway with Cindy (who was jet-lagged, sleep-deprived and nursing a sore leg after a long walking tour through Red Square), I saw her get up again and again to offer her seat to others. This is the servant's posture.

Learning How to Serve

When I first began to notice the need around me in the halls of my high school, I had a growing sense that I had to do something about it. (I should note that it wasn't a heavy sense of duty, but more like a hopeful, antsy desire to get moving.) But what exactly was I to do? I had no experience in being salt and light. The call to serve is often hard, risky and humbling, but thankfully it's not usually very complex. It's simple: as you wish that others would do to you . . .

Well, if I were lonely and excluded, I'd want someone to notice me, to say hi. So I began smiling and saying hi to Dean whenever I passed him. In this small way, I tried to serve him. This was really the extent of it until the day I passed Dean in the hall after school as I was rushing off to tennis practice. I said my usual "Hi, Dean," and Dean said, "Nice knowing you, Don."

I kept right on going, but right before I got to the tennis courts, God stopped me in my tracks. He said, "Let's go!" Meaning, let's go after Dean. The voice wasn't audible, but it couldn't have been clearer. I wanted to go to practice, but God was pretty insistent, so I ran back into the halls, looking for Dean. To be honest, I felt silly and foolish running with my arms loaded with a backpack and tennis rackets—I was more accustomed to trying to walk dignified (and hopefully ignored) through the halls.

But God's words were clear, and so I ran on. I didn't find Dean until I got clear over to the other side of the high school. As I ran up to him shouting, "Dean!" I realized I didn't know what I was going to say to him. This is where Jesus' servant advice came in handy again: As you wish that others would do to you . . . Well, if I were outcast, I'd want to be invited to do something. So, that's what I did. I invited Dean to come to dinner with some friends and me that night.

He looked shocked. (I'm pretty sure not many people ran after him shouting his name, wanting to invite him to dinner.) After an oddly long pause, he managed a small smile and said, "Sure."

Dean did come to dinner, and my friends were kind to him. He didn't say much during dinner, but later that week we hung out again. Dean divulged that on the day I stopped him in the halls, he had a pocketful of pills and was planning on taking them (and his life) when he got home. I was shocked. And initially my instinct was to run, thinking, These are some dirty feet someone else is going to have to wash. Yet Jesus had left me an example. So I grabbed the towel and basin and followed my instincts.

If I were desperate enough to try something like suicide, I'd want someone to nose into my life and help me get some handles. So that's what I did. We talked; we prayed; I helped Dean look for help. When he was eventually put into a psych ward for a time, I knew unambiguously what I would want done for me if I were in there. So I went and visited him. I sat in an awkward psych-ward visiting room with Dean as he tried to make sense of his life.

When later that year, after being released, Dean relapsed and locked himself in his house and we could see him through the window, lying unconscious, well, I knew what I'd want done for me if I were in that situation. So I smashed a window with my hand so we could get in there and help him.

I cut my hand pretty badly that day. In fact, I still have a scar. It's nothing like the scars Jesus got on his hands, of course, but I got it in a similar way—serving the needs of those around me. Before becoming a Christian, I barely talked with anyone in my high school. I avoided people and, during my freshman year, ate every single lunch alone. (That's not an exaggeration, unfortunately.) But once I became a Christian, this started changing. I was slowly developing Sober Eyes and Servant Hands. I was getting caught up in what God was doing around me. I was slowly becoming a more missional Christian.

Those first attempts at foot-washing were just the beginning. Every year I have gotten more caught up in God's mission, which

Practicing Fasting

I used to think that fasting was an obscure spiritual discipline that had little to do with today's Christians. For a Safe Christian, giving up food for a day couldn't be more random and unintelligible. But for the Missional Christian, it turns out fasting is an important discipline to practice. Self-denial is a foreign posture for many of us, but it is implicit in the life of a servant. In this way fasting is a very relevant discipline for those who are becoming more missional. It is something Jesus assumed his followers would do (see, for example, Matthew 6:16-18), and it helps us more fully learn the form of a servant. For those who've never fasted before, Lynn Babb's *Fasting: Spiritual Freedom Beyond Our Appetites* is a good place to start. Also, Richard J. Foster has a very helpful chapter on this practice in his *Celebration of Discipline: The Path to Spiritual Growth*.

means I see more need and wash more dirty feet. This missional posture has resulted in some of the most interesting, awkward, costly, rewarding moments of my life. Though I am still very much an introvert and hesitant by temperament, God has slowly been changing me from a frightened boy who hid from the world to a Christian who serves others in risky ways—even when being a servant has meant growing more generous with my money and more vocal about Jesus. In our day and age, those two expressions of servanthood deserve a little more comment.

Serving with My Resources

Washing feet often involves spending my time and energy on others. But sometimes being a servant involves generosity with my resources. This is the case for every Christian, but even more so for those of us who have been blessed by God with excess resources.

John the Baptist stated this obvious fact about service quite plainly: "Whoever has two tunics is to share with him who has none, and whoever has food is to do likewise" (Luke 3:11). This call to generosity makes sense. If it were cold out and I had no coat but you had two, I sure know what I would have you do with your extra coat! And so washing dirty feet sometimes involves generosity with our things. Giving our money and possessions away may look radical, but it is something we are called to do with our Servant Hands.

Jesus was clear on this matter: "And if anyone would sue you and take your tunic, let him have your cloak as well. And if anyone forces you to go one mile, go with him two miles. Give to the one who begs from you, and do not refuse the one who would borrow from you" (Matthew 5:40-42). Jesus does not invite his followers to serve with their time and energy but remain misers with their money; the call to servanthood is a comprehensive one.

Is it any surprise that there was an outpouring of financial gen-

erosity among the first Christians? We read this about the earliest
converts in Jerusalem: "And all who believed were together and
had all things in common. And they were selling their possessions
and belongings and distributing the proceeds to all, as any had
need" (Acts 2:44-45). This is what one would expect from those
who follow a man who came not to be served, but to serve.

As one would expect, this is an especially important calling for
Christians who have wealth and live in a world where most people
live without. Jesus often taught about the dangers of wealth, and
Paul made sure Timothy was addressing this important issue with
those he taught:

> As for the rich in this present age, charge them not to be
> haughty, nor to set their hopes on the uncertainty of riches,
> but on God, who richly provides us with everything to enjoy.
> They are to do good, to be rich in good works, to be generous
> and ready to share, thus storing up treasure for themselves
> as a good foundation for the future, so that they may take
> hold of that which is truly life. (1 Timothy 6:17-19)

Serving by giving resources is not as simple as it may sound, of
course. There are ways that our giving can actually harm others.
We can't just thoughtlessly flick away our resources in the general
direction of need. We need to get involved, and relationally,
thoughtfully and wisely be generous with our resources.

We'll look more carefully at this in later chapters, but let me
observe for now that Jesus' servant maxim, As you wish that
others would do to you . . . , is a practical guideline for wise giving.
Not sure how to respond to the man who's panhandling on the
street corner? How would you want to be treated if that were you?
Not sure what to make of all the political refugees moving into
your city? If you had endured a war, lost family members and
found yourself plopped down in a foreign city that made very little
sense to you, how would you want to be treated?

While our giving needs to be thoughtful, relational and wise, it needs to *be*. Some of the needs around us in this dark and decaying world are physical, and so serving is sometimes physical. Sometimes washing dirty feet means being generous with our resources.

Serving with My Words

Sometimes serving means saying something. No matter how shy or reticent or allergic to gross exhibits of evangelism we may be, part of what it means to wash dirty feet is to tell others about Jesus. After all, if I were without Jesus in this world (having "no hope and without God in the world," as Paul put it), I'd want someone to say something. I'd want someone to tell me about Jesus. So, as a servant, I tell others about Jesus. (All of chapter seven is about evangelism.)

While considering our Servant Hands, it's worth noting that if I were wandering about in the darkness, trying to feel my way forward in life, I'd want someone to announce a little light into my life. If I were decaying, seeing my relationships and spirit and sanity and grip on life sliding downhill a little more every year, and if my ability to keep it all together was getting a bit more tenuous with each passing season, and you had some salt with you, something that could help slow the decay—I'd want you to rub some on me!

So, as a servant, I come alongside those who are struggling in order to minister to them and to tell them of the healing and redemption that Jesus freely offers to all who come to him. Missional Christians serve with their words in this way—but not just any old words. Even in our proclaiming we are to take the form of a servant.

For example, if I were a non-Christian and I'd been hurt by the church, I'd want you to take it slowly and naturally with me; I'd want you to build a little trust with me before bringing up something I've become allergic to over the years. So the Missional Christian, as a servant in an age of rampant distrust, takes his time. He builds trust, slowly and naturally, with those who are without Jesus.

And if I were a non-Christian who didn't understand a lot of Christian terminology, I'd want you not to use weird theological words with me. So the Missional Christian, as a servant, speaks simply of Jesus—even if this means she has to train herself to use a new palette of words that describe her faith.

And if I were a non-Christian who was stubborn in my familiar darkness and kept kicking at any mention of Jesus, I'd hope that at least one person wouldn't give up on me. I'd want at least one person who cared enough to stay with me, one person willing to talk, willing not to walk on eggshells around me all the time. So the Missional Christian, as a servant, is persistent in his witness. He doesn't give up easily on the non-Christians in his life, even if he takes some shots as a result.

And if I had real questions, real genuine confusion about the Christian faith, I'd want someone to engage my questions. I wouldn't want people to just lob preset answers at my questions; I'd want them engaged thoughtfully. So Missional Christians, as servants, take people's questions seriously. They listen, they ask, they dialogue, they invite their friend to an Alpha course (or some similar place), where they know their friend's questions will be honored and engaged. (For more on Alpha, a practical introduction to Christianity, go to www.alphausa.org.)

And if I were ready, if I had come to a place of longing to follow Jesus, longing to be one of his, I'd want someone to raise the question for me, to invite me in and to *show* me how to come in. So the Missional Christian, as a servant, raises the question for others and invites them into the kingdom, and shows them how exactly to enter in.

The Missional Christian knows that sometimes serving others means saying something. Even if my own interests tell me not to say anything (*This is risky! What if they think I'm dumb, or worse—*

a Bible-thumper Jesus freak? What if they have questions I don't have ready answers for?) I know it's not about my interests, but about theirs. And so, at times, I open my mouth in love.

Living with Servant Hands

Perhaps in a perfect world, we could spend our days using our Giddy Hands to tickle our every fancy as Happy Christians. And in a dangerous world, we could become preoccupied using Defensive Hands to protect ourselves as Safe Christians. And in some relatively benign world, perhaps we could be Successful Christians and use our Grabby Hands to lift ourselves up. But here we are, standing in a dark and decaying world as salt and light, with Servant Hands.

It turns out my first forays into foot-washing were just the beginning. The more caught up I got in God's work in the world, the more I found myself serving others—sometimes in the most surprising ways. Simply trying to "do unto others" over the years, I have found myself driving across the state of Colorado in the early morning, running alongside a highway in Eastern Oregon in the middle of the winter, eating more than my fill of pig-brain empanadas, handing a homeless boy my debit card (and pin number), walking through the slums of Buenos Aires and trying to direct a gospel choir. Being a Missional Christian has meant using my two skinny hands to wash dirty dishes, work on plugged-up toilets, hold a crying friend, write painfully honest letters, knock on lots of doors and hold the hand of a dying man. I will say this: the life of a servant is anything but boring.

Lest I paint a too stylized picture of all this service, it must be plainly acknowledged that there is great cost involved. Washing dirty feet is messy. And painful. And awkward. There's a reason the disciples weren't jumping up at the beginning of the meal, offering to handle the foot-washing. To live as a servant is to pay a price. It is costly. (More on this in chapter four.)

Nonetheless the Missional Christian, caught up as she is in God's mission, knows exactly what her two hands are for. And wherever she goes, there they are, right at the ends of her arms, ready to serve. Wherever she goes.

Which does raise a question: Where should the Missional Christian go? There are dirty feet everywhere, so how do you know which needy people to walk toward and serve? As our Sober Eyes see the need all around us, as our Servant Hands take to laboring, what exactly does that mean for the Missional Christian's two feet?

3

Ready Feet

As shoes for your feet . . . put on the readiness
given by the gospel of peace.

EPHESIANS 6:15

● ◆ ●

EVERY CHRISTIAN HAS "feet" in the sense that we all
make decisions about where to go in life and during our days.
Every year we make hundreds of decisions with our feet: where to
go on Friday night, where to vacation, where to sit at the meeting,
whom to walk up to after church, whether to cross the street and
meet the new neighbors. It almost goes without saying that if we
are to *go and do likewise*, it will involve some going.

Safe Christians tend to go only to places that seem, well, safe.
These Christians have Cautious Feet: they tend to avoid those
places downtown that they've heard stories about; they tend to
walk to the same pew every week, where they'll probably know all
the people sitting near them; they don't cross the street to shake
hands with the neighbors who just moved in.

Successful Christians, on the other hand, have Ambitious Feet.
They are willing to go places that might seem risky or new, as long
as there is some personal advantage to be gained. They may head to

those places downtown that everyone talks about—to investigate them for potential development. They might sit in a new row at church—to get some face time with that influential elder. They'll even cross the street to say hi to the new potential sales contacts—I mean *neighbors*—who just moved into the subdivision.

And Happy Christians, well, their Skipping Feet are willing to take them anywhere that sounds fun or promising or adventurous or new. Every year, every week, every day Christians make decisions about where to walk or drive or travel. Our feet are busy. And while we tend to make many of these decisions without too much thought, it would behoove every Christian to note that Jesus wants to be Lord of our feet. He happens to have some very specific ideas about where our feet ought to go.

He made this clear to his first disciples while standing, resurrected, before them in Jerusalem.

> So when they had come together, they asked him, "Lord, will you at this time restore the kingdom to Israel?" He said to them, "It is not for you to know times or seasons that the Father has fixed by his own authority. But you will receive power when the Holy Spirit has come upon you, and you will be my witnesses in Jerusalem and in all Judea and Samaria, and to the end of the earth." And when he had said these things, as they were looking on, he was lifted up, and a cloud took him out of their sight. (Acts 1:6-9)

Christian Geography

We're told by Luke that the disciples stood there staring up into the sky until an angel came and interrupted them. What must they have been thinking as they stared, watching Jesus ascend into heaven?

Perhaps their dreams and plans for Jesus to lead them as the Geopolitical Reigning Messiah were crumbling away within them.

After he came back from the dead, the disciples must have been thrilled, seeing that their leader could not be defeated by death. Maybe Jesus would rule and reign and defeat their Roman oppressors? You get a hint of their overwrought messianic expectations in the question they had just asked Jesus: "Lord, will you at this time restore the kingdom to Israel?" (Acts 1:6).

But Jesus didn't respond according to their Geopolitical-Reigning-Messiah Plan. Instead he launched Plan Ragtag. He let his disciples know that he was sending *them* to spread his kingdom. Jesus' church is God's plan for spreading his kingdom around the world. And he laid out the geography for Plan Ragtag right there before ascending into heaven: first Jerusalem, then the rest of Judea, then over into Samaria and finally to the ends of the earth. Here Jesus gave his church her literal marching orders: Jerusalem, Judea, Samaria and the ends of the earth. The implications of these geographic markers were clear to the disciples. Jesus' plans for their feet were unambiguous—and challenging.

First, Jerusalem. By calling his church to be a witness in Jerusalem, Jesus was calling them to begin right away, with the people right around them. The *urgency* in his call was undeniable to the disciples. *Jerusalem? That's where we are right now! So, are we on this witnessing mission already? I mean, do we just start talking? Like, right now?*

Second, Judea. By calling his church to be a witness in Judea, Jesus was calling them to move out into new ground, to initiate with new people and new villages. The *initiative* implied in his call was undeniable to the disciples. *Judea? Well, that's the wider region we're standing in. Dozens and dozens of villages—a few days' walk gets us to any of them. Some of these places we know well, but many of these villages and towns will be brand-new to us. Well, at least they're all Jewish, so we fit in around Judea. We understand them, and they understand us.*

Third, Samaria. By calling his church to be a witness in Samaria, Jesus was calling them to cross cultural barriers, to initiate with people the disciples didn't like, trust, or want to be around. The riskiness in his call was undeniable to the disciples. *Samaria? Um . . . Samaria?! That's a little farther away—quite a walk, actually. But geography is the least of our concerns. The biggest problem with Samaria is that it's full of Samaritans. Half-bred dogs! Dirty, lazy, evil, impure dogs. Don't like 'em; don't want to. Besides, we'd look ridiculous walking into those villages; we'd have no idea where to start. Unfamiliar ground, that. And we're not too sure it'd be that safe for us, to be honest with you.*

And finally, the ends of the earth. By calling his church to be a witness to the ends of the earth, Jesus was calling them to cross national, political and continental boundaries, to go far outside of what they knew, understood or had experienced. The unapologetically *global scope* in his call was undeniable to the disciples. *The ends of the earth? The ends? Of the earth? But we're just fishermen and a lawyer and . . . and we're more the provincial type. You see, we've never traveled that far away from our home villages. Just being in Jerusalem has awestruck a few of us. The ends of the earth?*

Yes, the ends of the earth. This phrase wouldn't have just drawn the disciples' eyes to the horizon and the prospect of faraway Rome; it would have rung unambiguous in their Hebrew ears. "The ends of the earth" was a familiar Old Testament phrase. Time and time again God used this phrase to stretch his people's provincial thinking, to draw their eyes to the horizons and remind them of their global role as his people. So Jesus wasn't introducing a new concept to his disciples.

In fact, Paul described his own far-flung missionary journeys simply by quoting from Isaiah: "For so the Lord has commanded us, saying, 'I have made you a light for the Gentiles, that you may bring salvation to the ends of the earth'" (Acts 13:47). And Isaiah wasn't proclaiming anything new either, just reminding the people of their global mandate, which God made perfectly clear from the very beginning. As God called Abram, he drew his eyes to the horizons, saying, "In you all the families of the earth shall be blessed" (Genesis 12:3).

All along God has been interested in his whole creation—every square inch of it. As Abraham Kuyper famously observed, "There is not a square inch in the whole domain of our human existence over which Christ, who is sovereign over all, does not cry: 'Mine!'" This has implications for the Missional Christian's feet.

Every Square Inch

The geography of Acts 1:8 gives us an ever-widening ring of circles. Jerusalem is at the center, and Judea is the wider region Jerusalem is within. Samaria is a little further away geographically—and miles away culturally. And "the ends of the earth" is the widest circle—encompassing all of creation.

In one sense, these concentric circles give us an historical overview of the spread of the early church. In fact Acts 1:8 can be seen as a sort of thesis statement for the entire book of Acts, a book in which geography and the irrepressible spread of the good news of Jesus are the key overarching themes. Read straight through Acts, and you'll first see the disciples sharing the gospel in Jerusalem. Then you'll see them moving into the rest of Judea. Then, with an insistent shove from the Holy Spirit, we watch in amazement as the disciples begin testifying about Jesus in Samaritan villages. And finally, as Acts marches on, we see the gospel spread further and further out, until we end with Paul preaching the gospel in Rome—at the center of the Roman Empire.

At the bare minimum, the concentric circles Jesus gives his church in Acts 1:8 are an historical prediction and a record of how exactly the church began: from Jerusalem to Judea to Samaria to the ends of the earth. But perhaps Jesus intended these comprehensive geographic rings to be a constant reminder to his church of his desire that they take the gospel into all of creation. Perhaps there is something normative in Jesus' inaugural sending of his church, something Christians in every age need to pay attention to, something that has specific implications for our feet. Namely, that we have Ready Feet—feet that are willing to go wherever God says.

After all, in every age God is interested in every square inch of creation. This means in every age Christians need to take seriously those people they are already in relationship with (Jerusalem), those people in their wider social circles that they don't know yet (Judea), those people who look and speak and live differently (Samaria) and even those who live in distant lands (the ends of the earth).

There was an important *urgency* in Jesus' call to be a witness in "Jerusalem," an urgency that every Christian today must still heed. How many of us are utterly convinced that Jesus is the "hope of the world" yet can't seem to muster the courage to even bring his name up when talking with our friends, our coworkers, our family members? How many of us are full of patience and mercy for the clients at the food bank we volunteer at, but have only gritted teeth and rolled eyes and sarcasm for some of our own family members?

So the Missional Christian has Sober Eyes that see the need within the circle of his very own family. The Missional Christian has Servant Hands, called to wash the dirty feet that are right there near her all the time. This kind of inner-circle "Jerusalem" ministry challenges us and changes us in ways no other Christian service can.

An unavoidable initiative was imbedded within Jesus' call to be witnesses in "Judea," an initiative that has implications for every Christian today. How many of us send sacrificial dollars and tearful prayers across oceans for reaching people who do not know the saving work of Jesus personally, and yet we don't even spare a thought for the people living on our own block who are in the exact same dire straits? How many of us admire missionaries who forge headlong into the jungle, heedless of dangers, to save a few lost souls, and yet we find it "too awkward" to bring Jesus up in a conversation at work or to walk across the street to meet the family that just moved in or to ask that parent sitting next to us at the assembly at school if she attends church?

So the Missional Christian has Sober Eyes that see the need in his very own neighborhood and Servant Hands that are willing to wash the dirty feet of people he hasn't even met yet. This kind of "Judea" ministry challenges us to initiate with new people, to knock on someone's door, not knowing exactly how it's going to go, to risk bringing up spiritual matters in a conversation. Initiating with people in our loose social circles in this way challenges us and changes us in ways no other Christian service can.

When Jesus called his Jewish followers to go into Samaria, he was asking them to risk much. He was asking them to go somewhere they had been told to avoid their whole life in order to serve people for whom they had only distrust and venom. He was insisting that they confront their inbred prejudices. So reticent were the disciples' feet to walk into Samaria that God had to send his Spirit and speak through dreams and visions to get Christian feet to obey his Samaria mandate.

How many of us today ignore certain parts of town because the people there don't look like we do? How many of us carry around prejudices and venom that make us avoid certain parts of town? How many of us gladly send our youth on spring-break trips to faraway beaches, but cringe when the youth director asks us to send our children into the city?

God is still interested in every part of town, which means the Christian who gets caught up in God's work in this world needs to be ready to head over to the mission field across town if God calls him. So Missional Christians have Sober Eyes that see the need in adjacent communities they're accustomed to ignoring. And Missional Christians walk with Ready Feet into those communities to

begin to serve. Crossing cultural boundaries and getting caught
up in God's work there challenges us and changes us in ways no
other Christian service can.

Finally, we must take seriously this biblical mandate to spread
God's fame to the ends of the earth. When Jesus called his disciples to be his witnesses to the ends of the earth, he was confronting their perceived limitations and petty provincialism with
God's heart, which beats in an unapologetically global way. How
many of us suffer from a kind of compassion myopia? How many
of us can name the last five movies we've seen in a theater, but
would struggle to locate on a map the five countries mentioned in
last night's news? How many of us wonder about, worry over, pray
for, dream about, and investigate and invest in God's work on the
other side of the world?

So the Missional Christian has Sober Eyes that aren't myopi-
cally focused on only her immediate surroundings, but that are
called (by God's mandate) to the horizons. And the Missional
Christian has Servant Hands that are willing to look not only to
his local, pressing interests, but also to the interests of others.
Getting involved in God's work in some faraway land challenges
us and changes us in ways no other Christian service can.

Ready Feet

Though in an average day or week or year we may not give much
thought to our feet, Jesus' geographic call in Acts and the comprehensive nature of God's work in this world means that all Christians need to take their location, and their feet, seriously.

This may sound overwhelming at first. Jerusalem, Judea, Samaria . . . and the ends of the earth? Just one of those circles of
mission is plenty to consider. But all four?

Thankfully, as we see in Acts, God isn't asking his followers to be
omnipresent. And he isn't asking them to choose between the four
spheres. Rather, he sends his Holy Spirit to call his people forward

into the specific square inches where he intends for them to be salt and light at the time. He called Peter to break cultural barriers and minister in Samaria. But for most of his life, Peter was called to minister in Jerusalem among Jews like him. After his conversion and a short stint of ministry in Judea, Paul was sent to his hometown, Tarsus, for nine years. It was only later that God called him to his now-famous, ends-of-the-earth missionary journeys.

The same God-directed dynamic tends to be in play even today. In any given season, God may call us to "major" in a particular mission field. But over our lifetime, he often has us involved in a few very different geographic circles. The immediate call comes from God—as he reveals his specific will to us through his Spirit, his Word and his church. But the every-square-inch mandate remains the reigning paradigm and scope of God's work on earth. This means many Christians find themselves called by God into a new square inch every now and then.

So, the Missional Christian needs Ready Feet. A Christian isn't meant to walk around life with Cautious Feet or Ambitious Feet or even Skipping Feet. But rather the Missional Christian develops Ready Feet—feet that are prepared and willing to enter into whatever square inch God might call her into. Notice that our spiritual armor as Christians isn't really "full" unless we tend to our feet. As Paul wrote, "As shoes for your feet . . . put on the readiness given by the gospel of peace" (Ephesians 6:15). Christian feet are meant to be Ready Feet—willing and obedient to go where God calls. God loves Ready Feet. As Paul quoted from Isaiah, "As it is written, 'How beautiful are the feet of those who preach the good news!'" (Romans 10:15).

If we have Ready Feet, we will be open to go wherever God calls us to go. My friend Elias grew up in Santiago, Chile, and God called him to be a missionary in Denver. My friend Jen grew up in a small town in Oregon, and God called her to live in the slums of India. This actually shouldn't be too surprising: if God is Lord of our feet and if we are getting caught up more and more in his work in this world, this sort of *going* makes sense.

Many Christians, like Elias and Jen, are called to one place for the long haul. But others, like Paul and Peter, are called to different places over the course of their life. In fact, many Christians with Ready Feet find themselves, over the course of their life, getting a taste of every kind of mission field: Jerusalem, Judea, Samaria *and* the ends of the earth. As each of these areas affect us differently, we find ourselves more fully orbed and robust as Christians. This has been my own experience.

With Christina and Dean, I got my first tastes of being a Missional Christian in a Judean-type ministry: initiating with new people for the sake of washing their feet. This forced me to take some social risks and put my reputation (such as it was) on the line to serve others. These initial forays into using my Servant Hands, while risky and somewhat scary, were life-changing for me. To realize that God had used me to keep someone from committing suicide was a stunning realization. And it made my Sober Eyes even more attentive as I walked through the loose social circles of my life.

Being ready and willing to take steps into this "Judea" ministry made me ready for a big challenge a few years later after my freshman year of college. I was attending the University of Puget Sound and my InterVarsity Christian Fellowship Bible study leader invited me to take part in the Tacoma Urban Project. This plunge into the inner city of Tacoma brought me face to face with my prejudices about the city and those who lived there.

I had grown up vaguely convinced that the city was dangerous and, well, sort of icky. But living in the midst of the beauties and challenges and surprises and joys of the city during this urban plunge not only changed me on the inside, it also began a decade-long journey of being heavily involved in urban ministry. Whether in Tacoma or Seattle or East Palo Alto or Denver, I was discovering that being called to step into "Samaria" to serve was a blessing I had never dreamed possible.

Somewhere along the line, I was also invited to spend a summer serving in the Yucatan Peninsula of Mexico. I said no—at first. I was actually pretty convinced God wanted me to go, and I wanted to go. But my feet weren't really ready. My hesitance came from my father. When I brought up the idea of living in Mexico for the summer, he shrugged off the idea; it sounded a bit dangerous, and after all, didn't I need to get a job and make money over the summer?

This is not an uncommon predicament—having feet that would otherwise be ready bound tightly by parental expectations or family obligations. When God says "go" and others say "stay," you are put in a real tricky tension. How we handle this tension depends a great deal on our specific family and specific culture. In my case, after much prayer and thought, I reopened the conversation with my father. Pushing the conversation further forced me to be more honest with my father about my spiritual life and passions—something I hadn't been very open about. Not only did this open doors in our relationship, I got to pack my bag and board a plane for Merida, Mexico, and all the adventures of the ends of the earth.

I found that going to the ends of the earth was as challenging and rewarding as serving in Judea and Samaria; it just challenged me in different ways. And it changed me in different ways. This initial foray into the ends of the earth launched another decade and a half of taking seriously God's interest in square inches that happen to be far away from where I live. Whether serving in the Yucatan, Argentina, Honduras, Russia or Ethiopia, I have been humbled by how beautiful and important these global partnerships are.

This has been the course of my own journey, and every step of the way I have found I need Ready Feet. This is what a Missional Christian's feet need to be like, especially when God's call is uncomfortable. Nowhere has this been more the case for me than ministering in Jerusalem—among my family and friends. Right now, this is my own cutting edge: God calling me to minister to my family of origin. For reasons particular to my own biography, I would much rather fly to Africa and ride a horse up into the highlands of Ethiopia to visit the building site of a new school (something I did a few months ago) than visit my own brother (something I am doing right now as I write). It's easier for me to bring the salt of grace and the light of wise counsel to non-Christians coming to our church's Alpha course than it is for me to do the exact same thing for my stepfather. This is making me appreciate anew just how important it is to have Ready Feet.

Serving Crossculturally

One of the challenges that Jesus' call in Acts 1:8 thrusts upon his church is how to relate with people who are different from us. God's work in this world requires a church that can relate, with grace, crossculturally. There is no place for cultural ghettoes in a church that is called to go with God into every square inch of creation. In fact, the book of Acts relates story after story of how the early Christians learned to apply the gospel message to their own crosscultural interactions.

While there are many things that could be said about relating Christianly with people of a different gender, a different age, a different race, a different nationality, a different class, it is of the utmost importance when interacting crossculturally to remember our servant mandate as Christians.

Jesus calls his followers to be servants. He calls us to look to the interests of others, not only to our own interests. He calls us to wash other people's feet. And he modeled this sacrificial servanthood in his own life. This much we have seen. So all that remains is connecting the dots: if the Missional Christian's service happens to take him out of his house and over to another culture, he needs to go into that culture with this same servant posture.

What does it look like to go as a servant into another culture?

Well, Jesus modeled this for us. Paul pointed out that for Jesus to "take the form of a servant" meant "being born in the likeness of men" (Philippians 2:7) For Jesus, taking the form of a servant meant "incarnating"—taking on human flesh and form. He became a human to the humans—to speak our language, to sit in our neighborhoods. This incarnational instinct is the instinct of a servant, and it is the model for the Missional Christian who is crossing cultures.

Paul followed Jesus' example, and he wrote,

> For though I am free from all, I have made myself a servant to all, that I might win more of them. To the Jews I became as a Jew, in order to win Jews. . . . To the weak I became weak, that I might win the weak. I have become all things to all people, that by all means I might save some. I do it all for the sake of the gospel, that I may share with them in its blessings. (1 Corinthians 9:19-20, 22-23)

Paul submitted his own ways of doing things to those he was serving. He incarnated.

What might this look like for the Missional Christian today? It means if I travel to your country, I speak your language (at least I try!). Even at the end of the day, when my brain is tired, I memorize, I conjugate, I attempt—for I am there as a servant. I bend to you, so you don't have to bend to me.

Serving crossculturally means if it's hot when I land in your country, but your culture frowns on wearing shorts in public, I wear pants. If your people are late-nighters (up late in the dorms) and I'm tired after nine, I drink coffee and stay up late. If a tie is expected in your pulpit and I don't own a tie, I go buy a tie (and learn how to tie it). Serving crossculturally means if you can't read, I stop typing and learn how to draw. If you are laughers, I learn some jokes. I incarnate.

While this call to servanthood is unambiguous, it also happens to be painful on many levels. Our instinct is to *do* things our way and to *criticize* your way. How many times has someone from a time-oriented culture criticized someone from a people-oriented culture for "being late," while the people-oriented folks scratch their heads and wonder how the time-oriented folks could be so cold and impersonal?

While it is often easier and less painful to insist on doing things our way, Jesus provided us a model of another way of relating crossculturally. When I was invited to spend my third summer down in the Yucatan of Mexico, I had recently grown my hair long. This may seem like a trifle, but it illustrates just how practical and how helpful this servant mandate is in crossing cultures. I liked my hair long. I had plowed through months of awkward in-between length hair and could finally pull my hair back into a ponytail. In Boulder, Colorado, where I lived, this hairstyle was very normal and actually engendered quite a bit of trust in others.

But there was a problem. In rural Yucatan, Christian men were

Practicing Submission

Although laying down our own rights and preferences is patently un-American, it is the way of Jesus. Much of our lives (prior to marriage anyway), we are accustomed to pursuing things how we want to pursue them. Ministering crossculturally, just like marriage, confronts us with this egocentric view of the world and invites us not only to empathize with how others see the world, but also to submit to their ways. The spiritual discipline of submission may not be our favorite discipline, but for the Missional Christian, it is an important one to learn about, and practice. Richard J. Foster has a great chapter on this practice in *Celebration of Discipline*.

very careful to keep their hair short. Longer hair on a man was associated, in their culture, with some unsavory connotations. I knew that it could be an impediment to our ministry to have a long-haired hippie leading worship and teaching from up front. But my hair looked so great. And it had taken so long to grow. I hemmed and hawed for a long time, but ultimately it was Jesus' model and servant mandate that made it crystal clear what I needed to do. If Jesus' taking on the form of a servant meant coming in our form, I knew I needed to follow suit. So the hair got left behind.

Jesus took the form of a servant, being found in human form. The Missional Christian does the same, deferring to those he comes to serve. And nowhere is that more applicable than when he enters into another culture.

Living with Missional Feet

The Safe Christian's Cautious Feet want to walk along safe, well-lit paths. The Successful Christian's Ambitious Feet seek out paths that will accrue on her resume. The Happy Christian's Skipping Feet want to skip over to any locale that promises pleasure and thrills and plenty of good stories. But the Missional Christian has these two solid Ready Feet. His are ready to respond to God's calling, whether that means crossing the street, crossing the tracks or crossing an ocean.

Jerusalem, Judea, Samaria, the ends of the earth. Each calling brings out different temptations, different challenges, different joys, pains and thrills, different lessons, different changes in me. This all makes me think that the healthy church is a church that is being shaped by and used in all four different geographic spheres.

Unfortunately, at times there can be infighting among Missional Christians. We can become so passionate (which is good) about the square inch God has called us into that we can wrongly begin to view any other Christian service as subpar. The urban minister spits in disdain at evangelism efforts in the suburbs. The ex-pats in Africa shake their heads at short-term trips to Mexico. Families who ignore their own neighbors buy gifts for orphans in Russia. Volunteers at the soup kitchen lament the dollars spent on plane tickets to Africa.

But in God's kingdom there should be no pride of place, for God's eye is on all of creation. It's all his, and since the curse of darkness and decay knows no boundaries, a mission exists within every square inch—whether in the city, the home, the market-place or the distant land. A deep love of place, the zeal of calling and a servant-hearted depth of incarnation (all beautiful things) can sour a bit when myopia settles into place and one certain square inch seems the only valid, worthy, commendable mission for Christians.

Thankfully, both our proud proclamations and our provincial hesitancies melt away under the burning biblical mandate, the pulsing zeal God has for every square inch of creation. We all stand at the center of a ring of concentric circles—each of which our Ready Feet could be called to walk into. This is why the Missional Christian needs Ready Feet.

I have found that wherever my Ready Feet take me, I am changed. I have found that being missional (something I once cartoonishly thought was about helping, saving and changing others) is actually changing me. The missional things I see with my Sober Eyes, the missional service I render with my Servant Hands and the missional places my Ready Feet take me have a way of affecting what I care about, what I think about, what I cry about. In short, it turns out that getting caught up in God's work in this world has a way of changing your heart.

4

Compassionate Heart

I will remove the heart of stone from your flesh
and give you a heart of flesh.

EZEKIEL 36:26

● ● ●

AN INTERIOR CHANGE IS unavoidable once a Christian starts to get caught up in God's work. When you see the needs of this world with Sober Eyes, when you humbly serve with Servant Hands, when your Ready Feet take you into various places where God is at work, your heart begins to change. This is unavoidable. The Missional Christian's heart begins to beat differently, long differently, love differently.

Jesus told us as much. He knew that whatever we busied our hands and feet with would begin to loom large for us, to affect our hearts. He laid this out plainly for his disciples one day on a small hill where they were resting together. He looked around at his disciples and said, "Do not lay up for yourselves treasures on earth, where moth and rust destroy and where thieves break in and steal, but lay up for yourselves treasures in heaven, where neither moth nor rust destroys and where thieves do not break in and steal. For where your treasure is, there your heart will be also" (Matthew 6:19-21).

Jesus made it pretty clear that wherever my treasure is, that's where my heart will be. Where I invest, I begin caring. Where I *really* invest, I begin *really* caring. My heart follows my investments. My thoughts and concerns and wonderings and passions and daydreams and tears flow for what I build up and invest in.

Investing Wisely in God's Work in the World

It naturally follows, then, that if I am a Safe Christian spending time and energy investing in safety, in security, in identifying potential dangers and strategizing about how to avoid them, my heart will begin caring about just that. My thoughts will be drawn to my own security; my heart will beat for safety; and my mind (when left to wander) will wander toward the same. Ultimately, Safe Christians' emotions rise and fall on the tides of their sense of security.

Successful Christians, who spend time and energy investing in this grand, impressive Statue of Self for all the world to see, begin caring about just that. Their thoughts are drawn to their reputation, their heart beats for opportunities to get ahead, and their mind (when left to wander) wanders toward the same. Successful Christians' emotions rise and fall on the tides of their advancement and success, and everyone's awed recognition of the same.

When Happy Christians spend most of their time and energy on entertainment and hedonistic pursuits, their heart begins caring greatly about how entertained and thrilled and massaged they are. Their thoughts are drawn to the latest gadget on the block, their heart beats for weekends and vacations, and their mind (when left to wander) wanders toward the same. The more Happy Christians invest in feeling good, the more their emotions rise and fall on the tides of their gratification.

These Christian "investment strategies" are quite common and attractive, but they are implicitly flawed. Investing in security, success or happiness leaves your heart vulnerable to uncontrollable sadness and disappointment. There is nothing so fleeting and out of our control as security, success and happiness. By investing only in these fleeting commodities, we all but guarantee our disappointment in the end. The tenuousness of what we've tethered our hearts to leaves us vulnerable to winds that are simply beyond our control. Thieves break in and steal. Time comes and rusts even my finest of toys. Things break. I fail. Even many of my hard-earned successes go unnoticed by those around me. So this kind of investment may seem great in the short term (security, success and happiness are very attractive), but it inevitably fails in the long term. This is what it's like to lay up treasures for ourselves here on earth.

But if I'm on a mission, busying my hands and feet investing in God's kingdom as a Missional Christian, my heart will follow right along—just as Jesus said it would. The more missional I become (seeing with Sober Eyes, serving with Servant Hands, responding with Ready Feet), the more I start caring about this world of his and his work in this world. This puts me (and my heart) on a very different trajectory.

Instead of tenuous hopes followed by inevitable disappointment, which is the ride Safe, Successful and Happy Christians seem to be on, the Missional Christian's heart experiences something quite different. The Missional Christian experiences deep mourning followed by a grounded, solid hope. This is an investment strategy that may be painful in the short term (deep mourning is quite painful) but ultimately pays off in the long term (there is nothing tenuous at all about hope that is grounded in God's work in the world).

Several years ago, when I was serving as a campus pastor, I was graciously hosted in my travels by a retired couple living in a beautiful house nestled in the Colorado Rockies. After dinner the husband and I retired to the large hot tub on the large porch. As we relaxed and gazed out on the calm, snowy landscape, my host asked me various questions about my ministry, and after a while grew silent. I didn't mind the silence as I took in the scenery: this fellow had built the perfect getaway nestled among the aspens. In many ways he had built the cabin in the woods my introverted heart had always pined for.

He eventually broke the silence by quietly telling me how purposeless his life felt. He had invested all his life, he told me, in his career and setting up his retirement. But now that he had "arrived," he felt empty, like he hadn't lived for anything that really mattered. The longer he spoke, the more it became clear to me: he was envious of my life. Even though I had barely two nickels to rub together, I had purpose and was part of something big that God was doing. A realization hit me that night in the hot tub: this missional investment strategy was, in the long run, worth it—even though in the short term it involved pain.

Deep Mourning

When I first started praying for Christina, I had no idea what was going on in her life. But the more I found out, the more my heart hurt for her. I thought my tender teenage heart had known heartbreak, but this was a kind of pain I hadn't touched before. I felt true compassion for Christina. The word compassion comes from a Latin word that means, literally, "to suffer with." And I did just that—I suffered with Christina. I talked and prayed with Christina, trying to help her find the right steps forward. I wasn't a detached spectator; I was in it with her.

Eventually I encouraged Christina to get involved in a support group our high school offered. Scared to go alone, Christina asked me if I would come too. I gladly went, but this only meant more pain. Not only did going to the support group expose my reputation (such as it was) to rumors, it also exposed my heart even more to the hurting in Christina and others. Turns out, whenever you invest in others, your heart always comes right along for the ride. Just like Jesus said.

To invest in God's work in this dark and decaying world inevitably means experiencing compassion, suffering with others and deeply mourning the darkness and the decay. The more missional I become, the more bothered I am by the darkness and decay around me, and the more compassionate I am for those in need. In this way I am becoming more like the Jesus I follow.

Jesus is often described in the Gospels as having *compassion* on the crowds—a word that means, in the original Greek, that his insides moved within him. In the pages of the Gospels, we see Jesus moved with compassion, we see him sigh deeply, and we see him weep. Jesus had a Compassionate Heart, and his followers were to follow him in this. As Paul wrote, "Put on then, as God's chosen ones, holy and beloved, compassionate hearts" (Colossians 3:12). Again, the good Samaritan is a great image of what we're all called to. When the Samaritan came along the road and saw the dying man, he had compassion on him.

No wonder Jesus said those who mourn are the lucky ones— they have Compassionate Hearts, hearts that suffer with others around them. In this fallen world, the alternative to mourning isn't happiness, it's *ignorance*, for darkness and decay are all around. And the more I involve myself in being salt and light in such a fallen world, the more I find my heart caring about just such a world.

When I spend time and energy on God's mission, my heart begins caring greatly about how that mission is going. My thoughts are drawn to God's movement on this earth, my heart beats for his kingdom, and my mind (when left to wander) wanders toward the same. The more missional I am, the more my emotions rise and fall on the tides of this world and God's mission within it.

I find myself daydreaming about food distribution, ignored kids, struggling marriages and my neighbor's aversion to the church and all things Christian. My thoughts are drawn to the eyes of the people featured in the news; my prayers begin to flow for people halfway across the world. I am bugged by injustice and by pain and by people who go unnoticed. Those racist jokes that I used to endure (or laugh at) suddenly rub me the wrong way.

And the faraway look in my coworker's eyes, that faraway, walking-dead look that I used to ignore because he so politely kept to himself—all of a sudden I find my heart is involved. I care.

Practicing Worship

I've found that when you get knee-deep into God's mission, worship takes on new meaning. Years ago I was visiting the Greater Glory of God Church of God in Christ in Seattle. Just reading the name of the church as I pulled into the parking lot was like a lesson in worship. But what I saw inside was even more memorable. I had been in some rocking churches in my day, and I absolutely loved the extended, organ-led, praisefest that morning. Partway through the service, I noticed a group of elderly women dancing up and down the aisles—absolutely lost in the joy of worshipping God. It was beautiful to behold.

After the service, one of the leaders of the church greeted me and asked what I thought of the service. When I commented on being so blessed by the dancing of the elderly women, the leader said to me, "Do you know why they worship like that? Those women have a ministry among gang members all week long. They walk the hardest streets of Seattle ministering to gang members." The elder looked me in the eyes and said, "When they get here on Sunday, they need this." I've never forgotten what I saw that day and the lesson it taught me about mission and worship. While the Safe, Successful and Happy Christians might find worship to be somewhat recreational, the Missional Christian, whose heart is suffering for God's world, needs worship.

His suffering doesn't seem so unconnected to me or theoretical or as mere gossip fodder. Instead I find my heart entering into his suffering with compassion.

All this compassion (suffering with) and deep mourning might seem unattractive at first blush. If the Missional Christian has a Compassionate Heart, do I really want to be missional? Perhaps blissful ignorance isn't so bad.

Investing in God's work in the world may hurt in the short term, but it leads to something solid in the long term: a solid, sure sense of God's redeeming work in this world. And that is a surefire place to anchor your heart.

Grounded, Active Hope

A Compassionate Heart is a different kind of heart. Once you begin investing in God's work in this world, you likely notice that you don't have near the attention and care and thoughts left for the vacuous news that used to so enthrall; you may have difficulty summoning the same amount of vitriol for the championship game that you used to; or you may notice that the summer blockbuster already came and went and you never really got around to seeing it—even though you had planned on going opening night.

I have experienced this somewhat dizzying reorientation of my own heart. I used to get such thrills from cleverness and silliness and the latest video hit on the web. I used to be fairly impressed with myself. But the more missional I am, the more impressed I am with this mission of his. I experience an emotional, palpable sense of grounded hope, because my heart is increasingly connected to God's inexorable work in the world rather than the vicissitudes and changing winds of our culture.

My hope grows as I grow more impressed by God's work in this world. I find myself impressed by his ability to care and encourage and support. By his ability to heal and redeem and fertilize the human heart. By the tools and systems of grace and strategy and mercy that his missional church comes up with. By the ways he has managed to use me and my two hands to produce actual good, whole, healthy things in this world. If God can produce real change and growth through skinny, hesitant me, his kingdom really is powerful! His work really is going to prevail in the long run.

The Missional Christian has a heart that experiences deep mourning in the short term, but becomes anchored in grounded hope in the long run. And that is something that neither moth nor rust can destroy, that no thief can break in and steal. There's something at once calming and exhilarating about having a heart anchored to something so solid. Paul had a sense of this, as he wrote in Romans, "Not only that, but we rejoice in our sufferings, knowing that suffering produces endurance, and endurance produces character, and character produces hope, and hope does not put us to shame, because God's love has been poured into our hearts through the Holy Spirit who has been given to us" (Romans 5:3-5). Hope does not disappoint when it is anchored in God's work in this world.

Not only do Missional Christians begin to see how active God is in the darkest corners of the world (which grows and grounds hope), they also look forward to a sure day when God's kingdom will be consummated fully. Our hope is grounded because it is placed not in our tenuous pursuit of safety, success or happiness, but, as Paul wrote to young Timothy, "we have our hope set on the living God" (1 Timothy 4:10).

Living in a dark and decaying world with grounded hope is a substantively different posture than living in this world with a posture of activism or optimism, defeatism, cynicism or pessimism. God's train can't be stopped, and when your heart is anchored to that train, you find yourself energized by hope. Our grounded hope becomes active in this way; it keeps us going.

Receiving a Heart of Flesh

The more invested my heart becomes in God's work in this world, the less it's invested in other things. So when thieves do break in and steal (or the neighbor kids come over and break things), I don't seem to care as much. It's just stuff, after all. My heart is indeed changing. This one fact—that our hearts begin to change as we invest ourselves in God's work—bursts one of the myths I used to believe about "missions."

I used to think missions were for people who greatly cared about the darkness (or the latest damsel in distress) and were thus compelled and launched on their mission by their red-hot heart for the mission. God had "given them a heart" for the needy. And since I had never been "given a heart" for much more than my own safety, I assumed that those mission things weren't for me. Looking back, I realize I had everything backward.

Now I know it's the other way around. The more we step into the mission, the more our hearts follow. "Where your treasure is, there your heart will be also" (Matthew 6:21). If I invest in God's work in this world, my heart begins caring about God's work in this world. Whether or not I actually take steps to begin investing in his mission is just a question of the will, not emotions or "having a heart" for a certain mission. It's a matter of obedience. As Jesus put it clearly in story form,

> What do you think? A man had two sons. And he went to the first and said, "Son, go and work in the vineyard today." And he answered, "I will not," but afterward he changed his mind and went. And he went to the other son and said the same. And he answered, "I go, sir," but did not go. Which of the two did the will of his father? (Matthew 21:28-31)

The first son didn't seem to "have a heart" for working in the field; he told his father he had no intentions of going. But he was obedient and went. Even though the second son seemed red hot

(I'll go, sir!), he never went. Going into the field is a simple matter of obedience, not heart. The heart, as we've seen, follows right along. "Where your treasure is, there your heart will be also."

As the minister of outreach at my church, I help oversee our work in local evangelism and urban and global missions. In that role I have had a few people from the church come to me to confess that God has never given them a heart for missions or that local evangelism just doesn't get them fired up. Their words come across as half confession, half defense. My response is almost always the same: try it. Put your hand to the plow, and you'll see. As we invest in God's work in the world, our heart seems to come right along for the ride.

This change in the heart is a profound miracle to consider. The prophet Ezekiel foretold a day when God would change his people on the inside: "I will remove the heart of stone from your flesh and give you a heart of flesh" (Ezekiel 36:26). And this is precisely what happens when we get caught up in God's work in the world.

Living with a Compassionate Heart

I have found that living with a heart of flesh tends to draw some odd looks from the people around me. Missional Christians care in weird ways about seemingly weird things. And what so enraptures others doesn't hold the same weight with us. Those things that make God's heart beat begin to resonate within us more strongly.

I used to spend my time thinking about whether or not it was a "good TV night." Now I spend my time enthralled by this inexorable mission God has been on for hundreds of years and which I, myself, get to be a part of. Now I spend my time thinking about how suburbia could replace its grass with tiny fields of edible yard coverings. I spend my time thinking about how little attention it takes to make a difference for an orphan, a prisoner, an elderly man down the block that I never used to notice.

Because of this, some people have begun to look at me with strange looks. People who knew me early in high school grasp for a familiar title or paradigm or box to put me in. I've obviously become philanthropic or kind or an activist. But all these titles fall off me like old sticky notes. They don't stick. They don't fit. They aren't right. I know myself. I'm not really all that kind, and I can't even type philanthropic without right-clicking it to find out how it's spelled.

In one sense I think the way people are beginning to look at me is how I used to look at that rare species of Christians called "missionaries." They see me as other, as different, as a khaki-wearing Christian knight who's obviously made of different stuff than they are. But I'm just me—a Missional Christian with Sober Eyes, Servant Hands, Ready Feet and an increasingly Compassionate Heart.

And the net result of all this? I find myself hungry for God. My soul clings to God more intensely than ever before. So before leaving this anatomy of the Missional Christian, it's important that we pay a visit to the soul.

5

Joyful Soul

Whoever loses his life for my sake
and the gospel's will save it.

MARK 8:35

● ● ●

BECOMING MORE MISSIONAL has changed how I
live in and experience this world. It's changed how I see the world
around me and my overall posture toward it. It's even changed
what parts of this world I find myself in. And my heart is slowly
becoming less stonelike and more fleshlike.

By God's grace I have experienced changes in all these ways.
But I've also begun to notice that something else, something deep
within me, is shifting. My very soul has begun to be missional. It
seems the longer I am caught up in God's work in this world, the
more I relate with God himself differently.

All Christians relate with God in some fashion, of course.
Prayer, worship, the reading and study of Scripture have all been
a part of my life as a Christian from the beginning. As a Safe
Christian I was quite taken with the quiet, calm, familiar cadences
of Christian spirituality. The introspective and the contemplative
made sense to me. The hymns of the holidays sounded just right,

just as they should. The anonymity of a back pew was comforting.

Successful Christians, I have noticed over the years, are drawn to a different spiritual posture. It turns out it's possible to relate with God much as they relate to his world: with a hunger for success. Church can become another place to climb, another place to get noticed, another place to outperform, to impress. And the preacher's sermons often give tasks to perform, lists to accomplish, and Successful Christians can busy their Aggressive Hands performing for the most important judge of all.

The Happy Christian doesn't have to look hard these days to find a version of the gospel that makes the Christian life with God sound pretty much like Disneyland. God wants to meet my needs, satisfy me and see to my every enjoyment—here on earth and in the afterlife. Yes, Christians relate with God in a variety of ways. But there's something about getting caught up in his work that has changed forever how I relate with him.

Picking Up Your Cross

To fully understand how a Missional Christian relates with God, it is first necessary to understand just how difficult being a Missional Christian is. To be quite blunt, for me, getting caught up in God's work in this world has been painful. And uncomfortable. And awkward. And challenging.

Having Sober Eyes means that I am disabused of a comfortable ignorance about the needs all around me. Mourning is painful and exhausting. Learning to live with Servant Hands is humbling and costly, and has shown me with crystal clarity my own limitations and selfishness. Having two Ready Feet takes me to places that I'm not accustomed to, places that are uncomfortable, places where I have to risk much and learn much. And going through life with a Compassionate Heart, as we've seen, means suffering with others.

While Safe, Successful and Happy Christians may go out of their way to avoid suffering, pain and weakness, these are right smack-dab in the middle of the Missional Christian's path. The path of suffering was one Jesus himself chose. And this has implications for those who would follow after him.

When Peter tried to lure Jesus off this path of suffering, Jesus knew it was time to make the necessity of suffering perfectly clear to his followers. "And calling the crowd to him with his disciples, he said to them, 'If anyone would come after me, let him deny himself and take up his cross and follow me. For whoever would save his life will lose it, but whoever loses his life for my sake and the gospel's will save it'" (Mark 8:34-35).

The only way to save your life is to lose it. Jesus not only taught this, he lived it. As the author of Hebrews reflected back on Jesus' chosen path of suffering, he noted that it was "for the joy" that Jesus willingly walked into suffering (Hebrews 12:2). This cruciform way of life is our model. Jesus "founded and perfected" this life that we are called into (Hebrews 12:2), and he made it unambiguous that he intends us to follow in his footsteps. He couldn't have been more unambiguous about this:

> If the world hates you, know that it has hated me before it hated you. If you were of the world, the world would love you as its own; but because you are not of the world, but I chose you out of the world, therefore the world hates you. Remember the word that I said to you: "A servant is not greater than his master." If they persecuted me, they will also persecute you. (John 15:18-20)

When Jesus first started sending his disciples out to partner with him in his work, he wanted them to go out with eyes wide open, understanding that this work would mean suffering. In his "pep talk" before sending them out, he gave them a bracing and clarifying image: "Go your way; behold, I am sending you out as lambs in the midst of wolves" (Luke 10:3).

Can you see it? *Lambs* in the midst of wolves. Jesus was perfectly clear. Why should it be surprising or odd to us, then, when our steps into God's work are likewise difficult? "Pick up your cross" was a pretty simple, plain image in Jesus' day that shouldn't be lost on us. Safe, Successful and Happy Christians are allergic to such suffering, which is why Christians in every age need to be reminded of the need to pick up our crosses.

Timothy needed such a reminder. Paul, writing to his young protégé, mentioned his own suffering three separate times in his second letter to Timothy, and he encouraged Timothy to enter into the same: "share in suffering for the gospel" (2 Timothy 1:8); "share in suffering as a good soldier of Christ Jesus" (2:3); "as for you, always be sober-minded, endure suffering" (4:5). And Peter, writing to exiles who were taking it on the chin, was careful to write, "Beloved, do not be surprised at the fiery trial when it comes upon you to test you, as though something strange were happening to you. But rejoice insofar as you share Christ's sufferings" (1 Peter 4:12-13).

So I should not have been surprised over the years to find out that getting caught up in God's work in this world would be painful. But I was. And you know what else has come as a surprise? This suffering has completely changed how I relate with God.

Abiding in the Vine and Bearing Fruit

The more missional I become, the richer my relationship with God seems to grow. I'm not sure why that has been so surprising to me, but it has. I know Jesus said that if we lose our lives, we really find life. I just didn't anticipate the gritty, desperate, fulfilling, intimate, joyful relationship with God that comes with the missional life. But that's exactly what I've experienced. The more I step into God's work in the world—and consequently into the inevitable suffering that it brings—the more desperate I am for God. This desperation has become the fertile soil for a rich life with God.

In my first decade as a Christian, I would often write out my prayers to God in journals. As I scan back over those journals, I notice an interesting trend in them: in those seasons when I was more actively serving others (say, down in Mexico for the first time or living in the inner city), my prayers seemed to take on a richer hue, a more vibrant vocabulary of both praise and frustration, and an unmistakable intimacy.

I don't want to overstate it. It's not like my soul felt elegant or lofty. Rather, in those seasons my soul seemed to grow more hungry for God. Thirsty for him. This is, perhaps, something of the manner of relationship that Jesus was getting at during his last meal with his disciples, right before his crucifixion. "I am the vine; you are the branches," he said to them. "Whoever abides in me and I in him, he it is that bears much fruit, for apart from me you can do nothing" (John 15:5). Jesus is the vine that is rooted, that has nutrients. And his people are the branches.

On the one hand, this image implies that we branches have a purpose. Branches exist to produce fruit. Branches aren't on a tree to be kept safe or entertained or complimented. They are, in that sense, missional.

On the other hand, there's something about that verb Jesus uses: *abide*. In a short period during this last meal together, Jesus repeated this strong verb at least eleven times. Abide in me, abide in me, abide in me. Our fruit-bearing purpose and our abiding in Jesus are somehow connected.

This is very much akin to what I've experienced as I step out into God's world. I'm like a branch—simple, brown wood, utterly dependent on the vine for sustenance and juice and life. Abiding in him is the only way forward. Abiding is not optional or recreational or something I grudgingly do. It's needed. It's sustenance. It's not possible to be a Missional Christian without it. This missionally fueled dependency on God is quite sublime (though messy) to experience. Paul experienced it, as we read in his second letter to the church in Corinth:

But he said to me, "My grace is sufficient for you, for my power is made perfect in weakness." Therefore I will boast all the more gladly of my weaknesses, so that the power of Christ may rest upon me. For the sake of Christ, then, I am content with weaknesses, insults, hardships, persecutions, and calamities. For when I am weak, then I am strong. (2 Corinthians 12:9-10)

My friend Dan experienced this joyful paradox as well. Dan and I, along with a dozen other friends, were living in the inner city of Denver for a summer. We were working long hours at the Sun Valley Youth Center, volunteering with Sun Valley Community Church. Midway through the summer, we loaded a bus with almost one hundred kids and headed up to the mountains for a weeklong camp.

Dan was, like many of us, already exhausted when we arrived in camp. To top it off, he had a cabin of younger children—most of whom had never been out of the city, many of whom had emotional and behavioral problems. We hadn't been in the camp more than two hours before one of Dan's kids acted out. Dan wondered why the young boy was taking so long in the public restroom and went in to find out. Out of his own hurts and disorientation, the boy had taken his own waste and rubbed it all over himself, and all over the walls and floor of the bathroom.

Dan was a bright student. He was doing brilliant work in economics at the university. He was popular, friendly and athletic. And standing there in the middle of a dingy, foul bathroom, he lost it. His strength wasn't enough anymore. His heart didn't care enough anymore. His character was insufficient for the moment. This caused Dan, as he told us later, to fling his tattered soul upon Jesus in ways he never had before. "For when I am weak, then I am strong." That's how Paul put it. That's what Dan experienced.

He told me later, with tears in his eyes, that the most profound worship experience he had ever had in his life was the hour he spent on his knees scrubbing human waste from a dingy camp restroom. Dan shook his head at the wonder of it, the paradox of it. He had experienced firsthand what Jesus stated so plainly, "Whoever loses his life for my sake and the gospel's will save it." The path of suffering leads to intimacy with God. And this means joy.

This means we can get involved in God's work in the world because God is there with us and we can lean on him. Jesus made sure his disciples were clear on this as he sent them out to labor:

Practicing Silence and Solitude

Unhurried time spent soaking in God's presence is vital for the Missional Christian. The Joyful Soul needs unhurried time abiding in the vine, resting in his presence, listening to his words. One of the best spiritual disciplines I have experienced for creating this unhurried time is the discipline of silence and solitude. Ruth Haley Barton's *Invitation to Solitude and Silence* is a great introduction to this often-neglected Christian discipline.

I must admit that I balked at this discipline when it was first introduced to me. It sounded self-indulgent and overly mystical and, well, kind of boring. So I rebelled against this seemingly self-serving discipline: after all, we're here to serve, not to be served, right? We're here to spend our lives on the needs of others, not to tend to our own needs, right? Well, right. Except that abiding in the vine is something we can't go on without. Jesus said, "If anyone does not abide in me he is thrown away like a branch and withers" (John 15:6). Without time spent abiding, our service will dry up and die. And then no one will be served over the long haul. So, for the sake of God's mission in the world, the Missional Christian needs to take time to abide.

"Go therefore and make disciples of all nations. . . . And behold, *I am with you always*, to the end of the age" (Matthew 28:19-20, emphasis added). We can go, because he is with us. The mission is fueled and sustained and made possible by his joyful presence with us. One of my other spiritual heroes, Mother Teresa, discovered that this intimacy with God is essential for his mission to go forward. As she put it, "Our lives must be connected with the living Christ in us. If we do not live in the presence of God, we cannot go on."

Being Pruned

As if bearing fruit in this world and having a messy but robust intimacy with God weren't enough, there is one more feature of this Joyful Soul that is becoming increasingly clear to me: the beautiful reality of spiritual growth.

Back to that helpful image Jesus gave his disciples during their last meal together: "Every branch that does bear fruit he prunes, that it may bear more fruit" (John 15:2). Mission begets intimacy with Jesus, which seems always to beget spiritual change in me. In fact, the more I lean into helping others, serving others, bringing healing to others, the more I get changed, the more I grow, the more I'm pruned.

It's a wise gardener who prunes fruit-bearing branches. Pruning off excess, extraneous buds and twigs ensures more nutrients are streaming toward the fruit—which, as Jesus knew well, results in larger fruit and more fruit. So it is with the Missional Christian: serving others brings the pruning shears to my well-developed selfishness; crossing cultures brings the pruning shears to my cultural myopia, arrogance and ethnocentricity; mourning the plight of the orphan brings the pruning shears to my overdeveloped sense of entitlement.

Ministering in my family confronts my unreconciled relationships; ministering on my block confronts my hypocrisy; driving into the city confronts the residual tight grip that fear has over me, confronts the latent racism in my heart and confronts the pleasurable smiley-face illusions that staying ensconced on my suburban island affords me. Traveling to the ends of the earth confronts my thin devotion to God, my pettiness, my hesitance to listen, learn, submit and operate from a place of weakness.

Every branch that bears fruit, he prunes. While this pruning, cleaning and tightening can hurt a bit, it is something my Joyful Soul has begun to expect and be grateful for. I need this tightening and growth, for my steps into mission have brought me into a more spiritually dangerous landscape than I've ever roamed before. This means I have a palpable need to grow.

Paul knew of these spiritual dangers, so he encouraged Christians to grow and mature spiritually:

> Finally, be strong in the Lord and in the strength of his might. Put on the whole armor of God, that you may be able to stand against the schemes of the devil. For we do not wrestle against flesh and blood, but against the rulers, against the authorities, against the cosmic powers over this present darkness, against the spiritual forces of evil in the heavenly places. Therefore take up the whole armor of God, that you may be able to withstand in the evil day, and having done all, to stand firm. (Ephesians 6:10-13)

Based on my experience, it would seem that the Safe, Successful or Happy Christian makes very little impression on the enemy, and therefore faces minimal spiritual attack. But begin to get involved in God's redemptive work in the world and spiritual attacks will likely increase. I've seen this reality played out again and again in Christians around me.

When I met Jessica, she was a sweet young woman who had always been as quiet as a mouse. She had two modes in life: quiet and polite when around strangers, silly and loud when around friends. I was friends with Jessica when she started getting caught up in God's work in this world. She had started leading a Bible study, mentoring younger Christians and learning about intercessory prayer. As her joy and purpose in life increased, so did the spiritual attacks she faced. We prayed through this one day, and afterward she made an interesting comment that I've never forgotten: "You know what, though? I'm glad I'm getting spiritually attacked. It means I'm doing something. It means I'm in the game. For years I was harmless, and the enemy never even had to worry about me."

Stepping out as salt and light always seems to have this effect: it produces spiritual growth and it brings increased attack. I have now come to expect this. I expect to get pruned by God, and I am thankful for it. I expect the enemy's spiritual attack, and I am not surprised by it. When my church recently started exploring a work among a people group that is culturally Muslim and unreached, I paused and prayed. I knew that if we went forward, it would mean growth for us spiritually. And I knew it would expose us to increased spiritual attack.

I find it thrilling that God not only calls us to partner with him but also prunes us, grows us and equips us for all that he calls us into.

A Thing Called Joy

I have to say that I find life as a Missional Christian to be so much more joyful than the safe life as a Christian that I once lived. Certainly, I am still tempted to be safe (or successful or happy, depending on the day), but over time I am becoming absolutely taken with this life of being involved in God's work. Living life with Sober Eyes, Servant Hands, Ready Feet and a Compassionate Heart becomes somewhat addictive over time. I find life as a Missional Christian to be richer and more rewarding and exciting than I had ever thought possible. Even though it involves pain and suffering and tension and pruning, it turns out to be so much better than the petty dreams of security I nursed for so many years.

Jesus painted a clear picture of radical service when he told us of the good Samaritan. Think about the good Samaritan: this humble man saw the need around him (Sober Eyes), bandaged wounds (Servant Hands) and walked to a nearby inn to get help (Ready Feet). Jesus painted this picture and then said to the lawyer—and to all of us,"Go and do likewise."

This is exactly what Jesus began to say to me in my early months as a Christian. And now, twenty-four years later, having begun to *go and do*, I stand humbled and amazed. Getting caught up in God's work in this world has healed me and grown me and brought me to a place of having a solid, palpable, sturdy feeling in my soul. That's the Joyful Soul. And I can tell you in all honesty, it feels wonderful. My soul was saved when God marked me by his work in this world. My soul has begun to heal by getting caught up in that work.

That's why I labor as I do, encouraging others to get involved with God's work in this world—wherever that may be. That's why I've written this book. This is, in the end, my greatest hope for my children.

I find it interesting that when two disciples asked Jesus for seats of honor so that they could have greatness, he didn't rebuke their desire for greatness. Instead he just corrected their strategy for getting it: "But whoever would be great among you must be your servant, and whoever would be first among you must be slave of all" (Mark 10:43-44).

Jesus was, of course, right. There is a "greatness," a palpable sense of purpose and joy and blessing, that blossoms within us as we serve alongside God. This is what it means to have a Joyful Soul. To have a Joyful Soul is to know that it is all worth it. It is a solid sense of peace that following after Jesus in his mission—in spite of the pain, awkwardness and suffering—is absolutely worth it. The missional path is a costly path, but it leads to joy. This is so much different from pursuing the wide paths of safety, success and happiness. These paths may be easier to walk, but they invariably leave us empty, disaffected, bored.

In the end, it turns out Jesus really does know what's best for us. He really did come to bring us life. And he really did show us how to receive it.

If you find yourself getting caught up more and more in God's work, you might find it helpful to have a sense of the core mission fields that lie before you and to hear some wise counsel as you take steps into them. Part two, "Geography," is meant to give you just that.

PART TWO

Geography

As we get caught up in God's mission,
where are we most likely to find ourselves serving?

And what's most important for us to know
about serving there?

6

Purposeful Family

And these words that I command you today
shall be on your heart. You shall teach them diligently
to your children, and shall talk of them
when you sit in your house.

DEUTERONOMY 6:6-7

• • •

MY FAMILY IS MY INNER CIRCLE. My whole family
(a conglomerate of the family I was born into, the family I am creating with my wife, and my inner circle of friends) is the closest
mission field I will ever be sent to. This is my "Jerusalem," the
center of the ZIP code I live in relationally, even though some of
my family members may live far away geographically.

Just as Jesus asked the disciples to be witnesses right there in Jerusalem where they were standing, so God calls each of us (at some
point) to get caught up in his work right where we're standing—in
our very own families. Standing as a Missional Christian within our
family circle may be the hardest standing we will ever do. But it also
might be the most strategic standing we will ever do.

The Need for Purposeful Families

It is helpful to remember that God invented the family. It was his idea. The family is a solid reality, a strategic tool, a blessed institution that God intended and is actively involved in. And, it is important to note, the family has always been integral to God's mission on this earth.

From the beginning God intended the special relationship between parents and children to be used for the sake of his redemptive mission on earth. At a very basic level, this meant that children were to be formed, mentored and trained in wisdom and righteousness by their parents. "Train up a child in the way he should go; even when he is old he will not depart from it" (Proverbs 22:6). But God also intended this special relationship between parents and children to be one of the primary methods for spreading his revelation and inviting each generation into a relationship with him.

As God gave his law to his people, he was clear how this revelation was intended to be promulgated: "And these words that I command you today shall be on your heart. You shall teach them diligently to your children, and shall talk of them when you sit in your house, and when you walk by the way, and when you lie down, and when you rise" (Deuteronomy 6:6-7). The primary place for teaching the Word of God is the living room, the road, the bedroom. Proclaiming God's ways and teaching his words is not to be reserved for the few, the proud, the ordained. It's clear from the beginning that all parents are called by God to be heralds of his good news. We see this clearly in Psalm 78 as well:

> Give ear, O my people, to my teaching;
> incline your ears to the words of my mouth!
> I will open my mouth in a parable;
> I will utter dark sayings from of old,
> things that we have heard and known,
> that our fathers have told us.
> We will not hide them from their children,

but tell to the coming generation
the glorious deeds of the LORD, and his might,
and the wonders that he has done.

He established a testimony in Jacob
and appointed a law in Israel,
which he commanded our fathers
to teach to their children,
that the next generation might know them,
the children yet unborn,
and arise and tell them to their children,
so that they should set their hope in God
and not forget the works of God,
but keep his commandments. (Psalm 78:1-7)

In the language of Psalm 78, if people in this world are going to "set their hope in God," parents need to "not hide" what has been passed down to them. In this way, God's work in this world assumes purposeful families in which parents raise their children in the knowledge of God. But God's redemptive work through the family doesn't just flow from parents to children. Often God's work in and through the family comes from surprising places.

This was the case with Joseph and his family. Joseph was the eleventh of twelve brothers and is something of a poster boy for ministering to your family of origin, however dysfunctional that family may be. Bullied and sold into slavery by his siblings, Joseph could have written his family off forever. Thanks to God, he became a wealthy, influential man in a foreign land. It might have been tempting, at that point, to never look back, to busy himself serving and being used by God. It's interesting to note that even when God brought him back into contact with his family, it wasn't a foregone conclusion that he would minister to his family. In fact, his brothers worried that he'd pay them back for what they did to him years before: "It may be that Joseph will

hate us and pay us back for all the evil that we did to him"
(Genesis 50:15).

In the end, Joseph was led by God not only to forgive and serve
his brothers, but also to serve the world through his reunited family.

> Joseph wept when they spoke to him. His brothers also came
> and fell down before him and said, "Behold, we are your ser-
> vants." But Joseph said to them, "Do not fear, for am I in the
> place of God? As for you, you meant evil against me, but God
> meant it for good, to bring it about that many people should
> be kept alive, as they are today. So do not fear; I will provide
> for you and your little ones." Thus he comforted them and
> spoke kindly to them. (Genesis 50:17b-21)

So the family has always been an important mission field in
many ways. Parents can serve and train their children; siblings
can love and forgive and bless; spouses can lead each other to salvation (see 1 Corinthians 7:14-16). The family has been and continues to be an important part of God's work in this world. And
this has unavoidable implications for the Missional Christian.

The Role of Missional Christians in Their Family

Because God is interested in every square inch of creation, at
times Missional Christians find themselves caught up in God's
work in their very own family, in the inner circles of their life.
This is most obvious for those with children: Missional Christians
are caught up in God's work in their household and with their
children. The parental role is one the Missional Christian must
take seriously.

But it is also the case, as we see with Joseph, that we are at times
called to serve our parents, siblings or other family members,
whether our service means truth speaking, forgiving or mentoring. This role isn't always obvious to us. At times our families
are in our emotional blind spots, and as such we are often slow to

see how we might be called to go as salt and light to them. Sometimes this blind spot can be glaring: While we find ourselves selfless and caring for orphans in Africa, we are petulant and sarcastic with our blood brother. While we have compassion on those in the chaos brought on by systemic poverty in Asia's slum communities, we have only anger and venom in our hearts for those in the chaos of our dysfunctional family. We have grace for those who suffer over there, but are apathetic about those who suffer at our very own Thanksgiving table. Commenting on the decline of the church in Europe after centuries of missionaries being sent from Europe to the rest of the world, the director of the London City Mission soberly observed, "We went out to reach the world, but we did not tell our own children."

When I was in college, I heard a sermon on the life of Joseph by Al Anderson, an InterVarsity leader, who suggested that it is possible for God to use us to "Joseph-y" our own families of origin. Now, I grew up in a fairly chaotic family, and I was glad to leave them to head off to college and begin to grow up and heal up. I was becoming more missional every year, but because of my emotional blind spots, I never considered that my own family might be a place God was at work, where he might be asking me to *go* as salt and light. So as I sat listening to Al's talk, I was conflicted.

On the one hand, I had been learning just how beautiful and joyful it is to be used by God to serve in this dark and decaying world. On the other hand, I had exactly zero interest in reengaging with my family. There was a dichotomy in my life. I was one person while on campus, at church, down in the Yucatan and in the inner city. I was someone entirely different when visiting family. On one strained visit to my father's apartment, he asked me, as we drove out to dinner, what was important to me in life. Now, you need to know that at the time I was utterly passionate about the gospel: I was leading Bible studies on campus, learning how to lead worship, spending weeks at a time in ministry in the inner city, contemplating a ministry internship. But my answer to my dad's question? I shrugged and said, "I don't know."

Often ministering in our families causes us to confront our blind spots and hypocrisy. Jerusalem forces me to integrate my life, to actually *be* a Missional Christian and not just wear a Missional Hero costume and cape while on that spring-break trip. Jerusalem means *being* salt and light, even when I'm sitting in my living room, even on my early-morning haven't-had-a-shower-yet stroll to take the trash out.

I recognize that to tend to our own healing there are seasons when God may call us not to actively engage our family of origin. There are times when God needs to use someone *not* entwined in the chaos and emotional webs to serve our family members. But there are also times, I have learned, when we begin to get caught up in God's mission in our very own families—even if that is emotionally difficult for us.

Mother Teresa, a Missional Christian who gave her life to serving the poorest of the poor in the world's darkest and most decaying, neglected corners, was invited at one point to give the commencement speech at a Harvard graduation ceremony. There was humble, diminutive Mother Teresa facing a crowd of educated, wealthy Americans. And her message to them? After describing her work among the poorest of the poor in Calcutta, she concluded with these simple words,

> And you will I'm sure ask me, "Where is that hunger in our country? Where is that nakedness in our country? Where is that homelessness in our country?" Yes. There is hunger. Maybe not the hunger for a piece of bread, but there is a terrible hunger for love. We all experience that in our lives: the pain, the loneliness. We must have the courage to recognize the poor you may have right in your own family. Find them. Love them. Put your love for them in living action. For in loving them you are loving God himself.

As we seek to do what Mother Teresa suggests, there are some important things to keep in mind.

Five Things to Keep in Mind While Serving Your Family

1. Your health affects your family's health. Much of our ministry to our family is the slow, marathon ministry of presence. While we may be "short-termers" on a mission trip to Africa, we are "lifers" when it comes to our ministry within our own family. And our presence as salt and light is intended to have a powerful impact on those around us. This means that my life in God is essential to my impact on my family, which means one of the most loving, influential things I can do for my family is be a healthy Christian.

I'm sure you've heard the sage advice from flight attendants a hundred times: in case of a loss in cabin pressure, put your own breathing mask on first, *then* put masks on your children. While this advice sounds a bit selfish upon first hearing it (what loving parent would put themselves in front of their children?), it makes complete sense. It doesn't matter how much you love your child if you pass out while trying to put her mask on her.

When it comes to God's work in our own families, this dynamic remains true: we need to tend to our own spiritual health in order to have any sort of impact on those around us. You can't give away what you yourself do not have. It is impossible to impart a vital relationship with God to your children when you simply bide your time in the pew on Sunday morning. It is impossible to help your extended family pursue health and healing when you refuse to look at your own "junk" and enter into confession, repentance and healing yourself. It is impossible to pass the stories of God's great deeds on to your children when you don't know those stories. As you grow in your faith, this will have an effect on your family. You will become a living testimony to God's good work. And the good news is, you don't have to be "done" or a saintly Christian to impact your family—you just need to be alive and growing.

I have a friend, Jeff, who recently started to come alive in his faith, and I have seen how his vitality is beginning to affect those standing nearest to him in life. Jeff's kids have a storybook Bible that he has always read to them at night. He confessed to me at one point that the stories in there were really the only bit of the Bible he knew. But now Jeff is reading his own Bible. He attended an Alpha course to learn about the basics of the Christian faith and is attending a Bible study with other men his age. As Jeff grows in his knowledge of the Word, his kids are being carried right along on the wave of his growth. Recently, with his father nearing death, Jeff was finally at a place in his own faith to talk with his father about spiritual matters. God used these heart-to-heart conversations to bring his father to saving faith just prior to his passing. Jeff's growth and health is affecting his family.

As we tend to our own relationship with God, as we grow in character, as we heal, as we see more fruit of the Spirit blossom within our own lives, our families benefit. Our ability to speak truth in love, to forgive quickly and to pursue reconciliation (all key ministries within a family) is directly related to our spiritual health. Henri Nouwen wrote a simple book about how tending to our own "stuff" ultimately helps us love others better. If this is a tender area for you or if you wonder if you'll ever be healthy enough to be used by God, you might want to give *The Wounded Healer: Ministry in Contemporary Society* a read.

2. You probably have blind spots. The difficulties of ministering in a completely new and foreign culture are obvious enough to most of us (we'll be looking at that directly in chapters nine and ten), but what often gets left unappreciated is how difficult it can be to serve in the culture you've been immersed in since birth: the culture of your family. This is the case partly because we become "homeblind" to much of what our families are like; if you see it all the time, you stop paying attention to the details. It often takes an outside set of eyes to point out what we stopped seeing long ago. (*Uncle Len is depressed? I guess he does drink all the time, huh?*)

Not only do we become homeblind, we also develop emotional blind spots. Especially for those of us with a level of dysfunction in our families, our own wounds and history can blur our vision and affect our actions. This is part of why, at times, it's hardest to love those nearest to us. As you get caught up in God's work in your very own family, this is an important thing to come to terms with. Some self-reflection and time spent looking in a mirror at ourselves can be very wise.

A few years ago, I was in my home office preparing a talk for an upcoming student conference. The conference was on the radical, upside-down nature of God's kingdom, and I had been asked to speak on the call to love others in community sacrificially. I was tracing the importance of community throughout the Scriptures (from Genesis, where "it's not good to be alone," to God's calling of Abram to "be a people," all the way through to the "city of God" being prepared for us as we see in Revelation). The talk was going to be a practical theology tour de force, if you ask me: an inspiring call to lay your own life down, embrace community and sacrifice for others. I was busy lacing throughout the talk stories of how God had helped me experience the joy of loving others when . . .

I was interrupted from my sermon-writing reverie by the ringing of the phone. I picked it up, and on the other line was Buzz, my stepfather. I sighed and rolled my eyes. I was short with Buzz, making sure it was clear I was busy . . . and Buzz got the hint. But before hanging up, he wanted me to know why he had called: my mom's birthday was later that week, and he wanted to make sure I didn't forget.

I was *livid*. Who was *he* to tell me how to relate with my mom? I was the son; he was the newcomer to the family. The presumption on his part, the nerve, the gall! I put Buzz in his place, hung up the phone and went back to writing my talk about the importance of community and the joys of laying your life down for other people. But the irony was too much even for me. Seeing the juxtaposition between my beliefs/convictions/love on campus and my impatience/judging/venom with my stepfather was like having a huge mirror held up in front of me. I was forced to recognize how my vision and my heart were tainted when it came to my family. Buzz was trying to make Mom's birthday special. And I *had* forgotten Mom's birthday the year before. I couldn't go on writing the talk. I called Buzz back and asked for his forgiveness. And I learned that afternoon that I have huge emotional blind spots when it comes to my family.

It's basic driver's education really: before changing lanes, always check your blind spots. To wit: before engaging in ministry within your family, check your blind spots. For me, M. Scott Peck's straight-shooting observations about the odd habits we sometimes acquire from our families of origin have been a helpful mirror for me. Don't read *The Road Less Traveled: A New Psychology of Love, Traditional Values and Spiritual Growth* if you're looking for evangelical theological reflection, but do read it if you're looking to gain some perspective on your own blind spots and odd family-related habits.

3. *Your extended family is a mission field.* Just as God chose to use Joseph to bless his extended family, so God calls Missional Christians (at some level) to minister to their extended family: brothers, sisters, parents, aunts, uncles, stepbrothers, in-laws, grandchildren and, yes, even stepfathers.

This kind of ministry can be tricky—and not just because some members live far away and we don't see them that often. It's tricky because with our families we are often called to minister through forgiveness (think of Joseph in Genesis 50). There is nothing easy about forgiveness and reconciliation and peacemaking. And we live in a culture where simply topping your bowl of venom with a sweet dollop of "But don't worry about it" and pretending to move on is accepted. Real forgiveness, simple though it is, is quite hard.

Truth speaking is hard as well, yet this is often what we are called to do within our families. While we may want someone from outside the family to do the truth speaking (I wish the pastor would tell my brother what a jerk he is), often family members are the ones with enough history to deliver the truth. Ezekiel was clear that if we see danger coming to someone and don't say anything, "the blood" is on our hands (Ezekiel 33).

My friend Jeff asked me if I would help him bring up spiritual matters with his ill father. Jeff was honest with me: he said it would be easier for him if I initiated with his father alone, but he knew it was important for him to be a part of it as well. God may ask us at times to go to a family member and speak truth in grace. And, frankly, there is nothing easy about that.

Mercy is another common ministry we have within our families: simply being with those who are suffering, holding a hand in the waiting room, looking after the details of a funeral, sharing a coffee and simply listening—not trying to fix anything. There are times when a merciful presence is ministry, and this often happens within the marathon of ministering to our families. Like Jesus' call to visit prisoners and those in hospitals or James' call to visit orphans and widows in their distress, there is nothing easy about a ministry of mercy.

Though ministering to our families can be hard and tricky, our missional instincts really do come in handy. *Sober Eyes*: Are you willing to see the need? Where is there darkness and confusion in your family? Where is there decay and chaos? *Servant Hands*: Our call is always the same: to wash dirty feet. Selflessness really is the model—and really is effective. *Ready Feet*: Is there someone in your family God wants you to initiate with that you'd just as soon not relate with? *Compassionate Heart*: At times we may try to guard our hearts with our families, but we need to suffer with them and enter into their pain. *Joyful Soul*: Yes, it does mean picking up your cross, and it does mean it's worth it in the end. In this regard, it's good to remember Joseph.

Forgiveness, truth speaking, mercy—these are all pretty tricky activities to be called into. Personally, I have found *Encouragement: The Key to Caring* by Larry Crabb and Dan Allender to be very helpful in negotiating some of these tasks.

4. Parents are meant to be spiritual leaders. We've already seen in Deuteronomy, Proverbs and the Psalms how parents are intended to lead their children, raise them in the knowledge of God, train them up in godliness. There are dozens and dozens more passages that say exactly the same thing: parents are intended to be the spiritual leaders of their children. Of course the extended family (aunts and uncles, grandparents and so on) are ideally part of this as well, but there is a special role that Mother and Father are intended to play in the lives of their children. While there is nothing shocking about this, in practice this can be quite radical— particularly in our contemporary Western culture.

In our culture, parenting is marked by consumerism and experts. I pay someone to teach my child piano. I drive my child to the studio and drop her off so the expert can teach her. As an "involved" parent, I come to all the recitals and cheer on my child—and I hire the best teacher I can afford. But I'm not the one sitting on the bench teaching my child piano. This has become the common parenting posture: I pay someone to teach my child soccer, piano and karate. I pay someone to fix my child's teeth, allergies and behavior. At times, this parenting posture bleeds over into the spiritual: I pay someone to take care of my child's spiritual development.

Of course the "pay" happens in the form of an offering on Sunday morning, but there is a subtle way that we are tempted to abrogate our responsibility as the spiritual leaders of our children. We check in our child at the children's ministry center, while we go off to have our own worship experience. We drop our child off at youth group and are thrilled to have a couple of hours to run errands. Of course there is nothing wrong with specialized children's classes, and youth groups are a fabulous (and fabulously important) part of church life. But there is something wrong with parents who see it as the church's responsibility to tend to their child's growth in faith.

This subtle form of spiritual delegation and the importance of empowering parents to lead their children have been brought home to me since coming to Bonhomme Presbyterian Church a few years ago. Bonhomme has wonderful children's classes and youth groups and such, but they have taken a strong stand in insisting that parents not deflect their God-given responsibility to form their children spiritually.

Several years ago Bonhomme's middle service (at 9:25 a.m. on Sunday) was the church's largest. The size of the service had plenty to do with the fact that children's classes and youth classes were offered only at that time. Parents would drop their kids off at their classes and then go to church. Senior Pastor Tom Pfizenmaier called that service the "handholding service": it was filled with parents holding hands while their children were off getting trained in the faith by someone else. Tom saw a couple of problems with this setup: no adults were attending Sunday school, and no children were attending worship. So families weren't "doing their faith" together. So Bonhomme made some big changes, starting with getting rid of the 9:25 a.m. worship service.

The results have been profound. I have seen the fruits of this decision in my own family. Not only are many more adults attending Sunday school themselves, but families are now worshipping together. In fact, Bonhomme purposefully provides no options for children and youth during worship services (other than nursery for those three and under) so that families worship together, so that children see their parents worship and pray, and

so that families can talk about the sermon over the dinner table
and as they drive in the minivan ("you shall teach them diligently
to your children, and shall talk of them when you sit in your
house, and when you walk by the way, and when you lie down,
and when you rise" [Deuteronomy 6:7]). A copy of *Parenting in the
Pew: Guiding Your Children into the Joy of Worship* by Robbie F.
Castleman is made available to every parent at Bonhomme. And
our children's ministry director regularly provides training for
parents on how to do worship or devotions at home as well. The
message is clear at Bonhomme: parents are meant to be spiritual
leaders of their children.

While this may not be the programmatic solution for every church,
every church (and every Christian) needs to wrestle with the ten-
dency in Western culture to hand our children off to others and to so
specialize our ministries that families are never together. Since
coming to Bonhomme, I have been personally challenged (even as a
vocational minister who trains and leads all sorts of people) to re-
capture the vital, active, involved role I am meant to be in with my
wife, Wendy, as the spiritual leaders of our three children.

Two books I've found incredibly helpful as a parent are *Parenting Is Heart Work* by Dr. Scott Turansky and Joanne Miller, and
Spiritual Parenting: An Awakening for Today's Families by Michelle
Anthony. As a minister and church leader, I have found the *Think
Orange* materials to be a helpful resource (*Think Orange: Imagine
the Impact When Church and Family Collide . . .* by Reggie Joiner) as
well as George Barna's *Revolutionary Parenting.*

5. You can grow as a parent. For some parents, fulfilling the role
of spiritual leader comes naturally. Folks who were led spiritually
by their own parents have a storehouse of memories, spiritual
rhythms and mentoring instincts to put to use now that they are
parents. This is part of how purposeful families are intended to
work: the faith is passed from one generation to the next. That
cadence we saw in Deuteronomy 6 *really is* intended to be central

to how the faith is passed on. Consider that just a few chapters later in Deuteronomy we read this:

> You shall therefore lay up these words of mine in your heart and in your soul, and you shall bind them as a sign on your hand, and they shall be as frontlets between your eyes. You shall teach them to your children, talking of them when you are sitting in your house, and when you are walking by the way, and when you lie down, and when you rise. You shall write them on the doorposts of your house and on your gates, that your days and the days of your children may be multiplied in the land that the LORD swore to your fathers to give them, as long as the heavens are above the earth. (Deuteronomy 11:18-21)

Sound familiar? The call for spiritual parenting in Deuteronomy 6 is repeated here and is echoed throughout the Scriptures. But what do you do if you weren't raised this way? What if you learned about the faith through a friend or church (wonderful dynamics we'll look at in chapters seven and eight, respectively)? While this might leave you with a great model for how to share your faith with other friends or how to spiritually mentor younger people in your church, it doesn't necessarily mean you know what to do with your kids. If this describes you, it's important for you to recognize that you can grow as a parent. If you don't have the rhythms, cadences and instincts of a Christian parent imbedded within you, you can develop them over time.

This has been my own story. While my parents did take my brother, sister and me to church (until I hit high school), we rarely discussed what had happened at church. I was not without spiritual direction and nurture as a child, but it was not the norm. On a very practical level, I can't recall a single time my father prayed with me as a child. This doesn't mean he didn't pray *for* me or even *with* me on occasion, but it does mean that it was rare enough that

I have no memories of it. So, now that I am a father, I'm not sure exactly how to go about that with my own children.

Is it silly that I—a minister and preacher, a former campus missionary, a Christian author—struggle with how to pray with my own children? Perhaps. But there it is. Thankfully, God is helping me become more and more missional all the time, which means even getting caught up in his work under my very own roof. I am creating my own rhythms, my own cadences in mentoring my children. For example, I pray with them every night before bed. And now when I forget to, my children call me back to their beds: "Daddy, will you pray for me?" Ah, this is how it's supposed to be: the rhythms being passed from generation to generation.

Bonhomme's children's ministry and parent training have helped me grow in this area, as has my wife, Wendy, as we enter into this most intimate of ministries together. My children have taught me lots as well, which maybe isn't how it's supposed to work. But as they are helping me succeed as a father, so I am trying to help my own parents succeed in their roles. And, not surprisingly, I've found reading to be a great help as well. In addition to the books I've already mentioned, I was absolutely thrilled to read the very practical *The Danger of Raising Nice Kids: Preparing Our Children to Change Their World* by Tim Smith.

Serving Your Family

When Jesus told his disciples that they would be his witnesses in Jerusalem, this meant that their ministry was right where they were living at the time. There was no "off time," when they would hang out and disengage from God's work, and then "on time," when they would get caught up in God's work in the world. Rather, they were to be missional wherever they were—including right there in Jerusalem. This brought an immediacy to their call.

The same is true for us today. As we get caught up in God's work in the world, it may surprise us to find out that God is at work right in our own families—and that he may actually want to use us in that work.

This was the case with Esther. As the chosen bride of King Ahasuerus, she lived in the palace and was presumably safe from the edict the king sent out that all Jews were to be killed on the same day. Esther's dilemma was palpable: do nothing and hope that the "family chaos" Mordecai and her other Jewish relatives were going to experience wouldn't touch her . . . or do something. But to even approach the king without being called for meant risking her very life. Thus Esther's dilemma. Might God want to use her to help her family? Was this worth the risks involved? Esther was undecided.

Then Mordecai sent a message to give her perspective. He wanted her to know that God would save her people, whether she helped out or not, saying, "If you keep silent at this time, relief and deliverance will rise for the Jews from another place" (Esther 4:14). But Mordecai also wanted her to consider that God might have brought her to her own place of health and influence so that he could use her in his plan to save her people. "And who knows whether you have not come to the kingdom for such a time as this?" (v. 14).

Sometimes that's how God works. He calls Missional Christians to be witnesses and servants right where he has caused them to be born—in their family circle.

7

Relational Evangelism

How are they to believe in him of whom
they have never heard?

ROMANS 10:14

• • •

WHEN I STAND in front of my house, I can see nearly my whole block; about twenty houses are in view. I know almost all of the people who live in those houses. And with a short walk, I can tour my entire subdivision, including my kids' school just down the block. I'll see some people I don't know on the walk, but many of them I'll recognize. And many of them will recognize me. This is my neighborhood.

If I go through the motions of a normal week—not going out of my way at all, just going with my normal flow—I encounter dozens more people who regularly come into my orbit at work, at the store, at the game, at the gym. This is my community. And my neighborhood and community form a mission field, a place that needs salt and light.

Just as Jesus asked the disciples to be witnesses not only in Jerusalem, but also in the villages of Judea that surrounded Jerusalem, so God calls each of us (at some point) to get caught up in his work in our wider social orbits. Because the need in our neighborhoods and communities is diverse, this Judean ministry may take on many different shapes and sizes: from comforting the sick to befriending the lonely to mentoring the young. For those of us who are accustomed to a more insular week (during which we don't interact with new people), this Judean ministry is just as important and imminent and challenging as Jesus' call to the disciples to go on to other, new villages in Judea.

But to be honest, as I stand here in my driveway, it can be tempting to conclude that there's not so much darkness and decay around here. I see nicely manicured lawns, well-kept cars, stylish families, smiles everywhere. But I know that looks can be deceiving. I know that smiles are often only on the surface. I also know that many of these people I see, people who smile and wave at me, are lost—alienated from God. That means that if I get caught up in what God is doing here in my neighborhood and in my wider community, I might find myself giving witness about the good news of Jesus.

Being a Missional Christian means being a witness for Jesus, even close to home. Now, for those of us who cringe when we hear the E word (evangelism), this just may be the hardest mission work we will ever be called to. Standing as Missional Christians within our neighborhood, workplace, classes or other social settings may be the hardest standing we will ever do. But it also might be the most life-changing—without ever even needing to board a plane.

The Need for Relational Evangelism

Back in the Garden, Adam and Eve sinned, and they knew it. Once so relaxed and at home with God, they immediately felt ashamed for what they had done. They were guilty, and they felt their guilt. In their palpable sense of sin, they didn't feel at home with God anymore, and so they hid from him. This is the ultimate plight of all of humanity: in our sin, we hide from God.

Sin has created a gulf between us and God. This is a real problem, and the problem is everywhere.

Sin is like a disease, like kudzu vines spread throughout all humanity, covering every last inch of this earth—including our neighborhoods. I can't allow the perfectly geometric shapes of our suburban bushes to calm me into believing that there's no darkness and decay here. I once happened to check on an elderly neighbor as my kids and I were going for a walk, and I found her passed out on her back patio, bleeding from a head injury. When the paramedics arrived, they told me if I hadn't stopped by, she would likely have died. That's become something of a parable for me: if I had God's eyes, I imagine I would see that many people living near me are spiritually dying. And they need help. They need someone to stop by and notice the bleeding.

Because of sin, we all need help. This is why, back in the garden (right there in Genesis 3, when the apple core hadn't even had a chance to turn brown), God started a rescue mission. He is on a mission to get us back and will do whatever it takes so that we can rest, at home in his presence again. This is why he called Abram and led David and sent his son Jesus into the world: to make a way for people to be cleansed, so that we can rest with him again. And this is precisely why Jesus has sent his church into every square inch of the world—to give witness to this good news. That's evangelism, a word that comes from the Greek word for "good news." Evangelism is nothing more than passing on good news.

Here's an important thing to note about this good news: God has not roared it from a megaphone to the whole world; instead, he has sent his saved ones as living testimonies to spread this good news. This is core to what it means to be a Missional Christian: we are not only marked by God's work in this world (he saved us); we are also caught up in that rescue mission—telling others about the good news of Jesus, telling them there is a way for us to rest, at home with God again.

While God's church does engage in evangelistic programs and crusades from time to time, and while there are some prominent and fruitful public evangelists (think Billy Graham), the bread and butter of evangelism has always been *relational* evangelism: friends sharing with friends, family members sharing with family members. This is the way the gospel is most fruitfully announced these days: in the warm light of friendship, trust and family. Certainly Jesus himself spoke to large crowds (and there will always be a place for evangelistic preaching and teaching), but he then called all his followers to be portable witnesses of the good news themselves.

Relational evangelism isn't the only way people hear about Jesus, but it is arguably the best. Research suggests that 70 percent of those who come to faith in Jesus these days do so through a friendship. It also suggests that the odds of a new Christian being vibrant in her faith a year after her conversion go way up if she came to faith in a context of relationships that will continue. Trust is the fertile ground within which faith grows, and trust is created through simple, unspectacular, everyday relationships. This has unavoidable implications for the Missional Christian.

The Role of the Missional Christian with the Lost

When the implications of Jesus' simple words "you will be my witness" begin to digest within our heart, often we are tempted to equivocate. Certainly, we reason, Jesus is talking about *other* Christians, not me. There's no way *I* can be a witness. Our rationale and hesitations vary:

- I'm pretty allergic to evangelism because of some pretty ugly things I've seen done in the name of evangelism. I will be no party to that.

- I'm not a perfect Christian, so wouldn't it be hypocritical for me to share with others?

- I'm more a behind-the-scenes kind of person. Words aren't my specialty. I think God should use those who are more gifted.
- I don't have everything figured out. What if someone asks me a question I don't know the answer to?
- It might be awkward, scary or risky to bring Jesus up in a conversation.

While we may have reasons to hesitate, the good news about relational evangelism is that our missional anatomy and instincts actually serve us quite well in this task. So if you've seen ugly things done in the name of evangelism, just go ahead and ditch those ugly models of evangelism and simply be missional with your friends and family who aren't Christians.

For example, Missional Christians have Sober Eyes, so we need to be willing to look at the people in our social circles with God's eyes and not be afraid to see the darkness and decay. The reality is, people are dying without Jesus, and there is no other way for them to be reconciled with God other than coming to faith in Jesus. This assessment of non-Christians is not judgmental or old-fashioned. It is realistic and loving. It is patently biblical.

As Missional Christians, we cannot allow the rose-colored glasses of our age to fool us into thinking life without Jesus is okay. It isn't. Right here from my own front yard, I can see the fallout of living alienated from God: depression, division, drugs, divorce, pettiness of all stripes and sizes. And the harsh reality is that this is only a precursor of what it will be like to live alienated from God in eternity. I see this if I look thoughtfully with my Sober Eyes.

Missional Christians also have Servant Hands, so we need to be willing to serve our friends who don't know Jesus and are alienated from God. Even if we'd rather not share with them, that's not the point: we are here as servants, so we are not here to look to our own interests (perhaps not wanting to share about Jesus) but to theirs (their palpable need for salvation). This doesn't mean we throw caution and sense to the wind and start pounding them over the head with a Bible, of course. We are servants. As we saw back in chapter two, it is incumbent upon us to share the good news how we would have others share it with us. "Do unto others" means we pay attention to where our friend is on her journey, and serve her right there.

Missional Christians also have Ready Feet, so we need to be willing to bear witness when called upon. When God nudges us, we need to be ready to share. Sometimes this means using our Ready Feet to initiate with someone new. If I'm to serve the people God calls me to, that means (at times) I need to be willing to go over and initiate with them. Just as the disciples were called to go into new Judean villages, so we are called to go and initiate new relationships.

- I go over to you where you are waiting for your parent-teacher conference, even though I don't already know you.

- I go over to the new cubicle to welcome you to the company, to see if your cubicle happens to be sitting in a square inch I'm supposed to be the salt of.

- I scoot over to the edge of the bench to make room for you to wait for the bus with me.

- I walk up to your dorm room door to see if you are heading down to the dining hall too.

- I walk one hundred feet to meet the neighbors I still don't know after being on this block for ten years.

- I walk across the mall to help you pick up your dropped bags.

- I walk across the coffee shop.

- I linger after the meeting a bit. . . .

The Missional Christian also has a Compassionate Heart. This means we must be willing to empathize with friends, to get into their pains, to feel with them. Evangelism isn't a combative sport in which we argue our "opponent" into submission. Rather, it is meant to be an emotional, relational, empathetic process. The conversion process is rarely easy or pain free, which means, as Missional Christians, we are willing to enter into the process with others, to suffer with them, pray with them, talk with them, be patient with them and celebrate with them.

And of course the Missional Christian has a Joyful Soul. We know that getting caught up in God's work in this world means suffering. It is costly to be involved in relational evangelism. But, as is always true in God's kingdom, it is also unquestionably worth it. As we lose our lives in witness, we find life.

As we go about this tremendous work of being a witness in our neighborhood and wider community, there are a few things that it would be helpful to keep in mind.

Five Things to Keep in Mind While Serving the Lost

1. God can use anyone. I'm not sure why God has chosen to work through imperfect people, but so he has. Whenever God calls us to labor with him, there is a knee-jerk temptation to point to our own failings and weaknesses—surely God can't use me! Abram pointed to his wrinkles—surely God can't use me! Moses pointed to his speech impediment—surely God can't use me! Gideon pointed to his woeful lack of pedigree—surely God can't use me! Whenever we feel that our weaknesses and failings disqualify us from being used by God, we need to stop and remember that weak and imperfect people are the only kind of people God has ever used. Sarah laughed in God's face. Peter denied Christ. Paul persecuted his followers. And God was able to use them all.

So, if you ever find yourself wishing that "someone" would share the faith with a friend of yours, just take a look in the mirror. Perhaps God wants to use you. My friend Adam recently came alive in faith after years of sleepwalking through life. Though his suburban bushes have always remained perfectly trimmed, the chaos of life and the darkness within brought Adam to a place of calling out to God for help. God answered him, and that's when Adam called me.

Adam and I began to talk about Jesus' invitation to life, and Adam quickly signed up for an Alpha course to hear more about Jesus. His life hasn't been the same since. Not only is Adam on fire for Jesus, he also has begun inviting his extensive network of friends and family to learn about Jesus too. But you need to understand something: Adam isn't a gregarious type; he is soft-spoken. Adam doesn't have an extensive understanding of the Bible; he is just learning the Gospels. Adam doesn't have all the answers, but he is being changed by Jesus.

And so, soft-spoken Adam is inviting everyone in his Judea to find out about Jesus. In his own way, he has invited parents, siblings, friends and people at work to come to an Alpha course to hear about Jesus. It's simple, really. This is where Adam's faith in Jesus grew, so he's inviting others to come and sit in that same place. He now helps facilitate table discussions at Alpha and has even taken over as Alpha's emcee. This should come as no surprise though: God can use anyone.

2. Your life matters more than your words. Adam is a lot like the blind man that Jesus healed (see John 9). As soon as he was healed, his eyesight was a witness to the power of Jesus, without saying a single word. Though Adam doesn't have a well-developed systematic theology, he has a changed life—and this is the kind of witness God can use. Adam has had people who've known him his whole life come up to him and say, "I see how you are different now. And I want that for myself." In this way, our life in Jesus is essential to our witness.

One day St. Francis supposedly gave this sage advice to some younger monks whom he was training: "Preach the gospel at all times. When necessary, use words." Whether he said it or not is beside the point. The saying is true: our lives give testimony to the good news of Jesus, even without words. After all, didn't Jesus say we are the light of the world? By our very nature, by being his saved ones, we are the gospel message lived out in four dimensions.

At one point in Boulder, Colorado, Wendy and I had a neighbor who was a professor at the nearby college campus. Sam was quite liberal and allergic to all things Christian. He knew that Wendy and I were Christian leaders on campus, and this became a large barrier to our relationship. But one late summer afternoon, after Wendy and I had been gone for eight weeks, living in inner-city Denver among the poor, Sam noticed we were back and came to the fence separating our backyards to ask where we'd been. I told him a bit about moving in with a Chilean family and learning from the poor all summer. He actually knew the neighborhood in Denver I was talking about (and knew how dangerous it was), and his eyes got wide as he began asking me question after question about our summer. Where my words could gain no inroads for sharing with him, my actions did.

This is often how it goes. When a concerned father recently asked me what he could do to interest his teenage son in the gospel, my advice was simple: do something inexplicably beautiful, risky and costly for Jesus. John Wesley once pointed out that if you want to draw a crowd, all you need to do is set yourself on fire. People, he observed, love watching other people burn. A life on fire for Jesus is a powerful tool in relational evangelism.

3. Your words do matter. While it is important that people be able to *see* the gospel in our lives, they still have a need to *hear* the gospel as well. Our actions are not always self-interpreting, and so we need to be able to interpret them in intelligible ways. A few years ago, my friend Tim and I spent a night going around the dorms at the CU Boulder campus, knocking on doors and inviting people to help us "free a slave." Tim had recently come alive in his faith and was getting caught up in God's passion for the poor and oppressed. So we were spending a Friday night inviting others to be a part of a campaign we were sponsoring to raise money for the International Justice Mission to help find legal remedies for those who were illegally enslaved in Southeast Asia.

We were advancing the gospel that night. But we began to notice partway through the evening that we needed to interpret our actions for others. Many of the students, when they found out why we were at their door, were moved and said something along the lines of "Oh, you guys are so nice." Tim and I were taken aback and looked at each other, a bit confused. You see, we had been marveling ourselves at how God could take two innately selfish guys like us and use us in this way. We weren't nice at all; we were being changed by Jesus! And so we realized we needed to interpret our lived-out gospel with words: "Trust us, we're not nice at all. We follow an amazing God who is passionate about the oppressed."

The reality is, the gospel is an announcement, and this means we are heralds. As Missional Christians, we use our mouths for God. As with all service that we render, we want to do this verbal service as well as we can. I have found that if Christians are not purposeful about their words, they inevitably fall into familiar linguistic ruts and use "Christianese" words and cliché phrases that don't mean much to the non-Christians they are trying to explain the gospel to. So, as servants, we need to be *purposeful* with our words.

We can grow in our ability to herald and explain the gospel. One of the best books I've read recently that has helped me replace my own clichés and stereotypes with more fresh, robust language that really communicates is James Choung's *True Story: A Christianity Worth Believing In*. I've also been told that my own *Jesus with Dirty Feet: A Down-to-Earth Look at Christianity for the Curious and Skeptical* is also useful to read for developing a fresh palette of clear words for talking about Jesus.

Having clear, simple, helpful words is very empowering. When I met Michelle, she was a shy freshman on campus in Boulder. She

called me after going to an Urbana missions conference because
she was feeling God calling her to be more missional on campus.
The problem was that, even though she lived in the dorms, she
rarely spoke with anyone, she said. We began a wonderful mentoring relationship, and one week early on I happened to mention
the Four Circles diagram found in James Choung's *True Story*. I

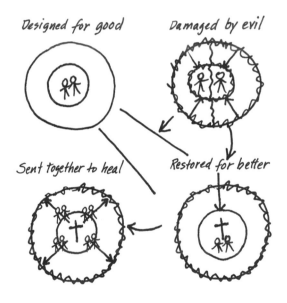

Four Circles diagram (From James Choung, *True Story* [Downers Grove,
Ill.: InterVarsity Press, 2008], p. 215.)

told her how excited I was that I could sum up the entire "Christian
cosmology" using four simple circles. I drew the diagram on a
piece of paper as I walked through the simple gospel explanation,
and Michelle was just as excited about it as I was. The next week
when we got together, Michelle mentioned how helpful she had
found these new words for describing the faith—so helpful, in
fact, that she had shared it with three people during the week.

I couldn't believe what I was hearing. Shy Michelle had shared the gospel with three people? "Michelle," I asked, "have you ever shared the gospel with someone before?" She looked confused. "Oh, I'm way too shy to share the gospel with anyone, Don." But then she realized that she *had* shared the gospel with those three people. It had been so natural and non-cliché that she hadn't even thought of it as "sharing the gospel." In this way, having helpful words is often freeing for the Missional Christian. Where clichés and stereotypes often stick in our throats, the gospel itself, clearly explained in simple words, naturally wants to be shared.

4. Evangelism is different in this "postmodern" age. For about three hundred years, the Christian church in the West has purposefully announced the good news in a way perfectly fitted to the modern era. From the 1600s on, the church in the West has been presenting the gospel to a people who placed a strong emphasis on human reasoning (Does the gospel make rational sense?), who thought in individualistic categories (How does the gospel affect me?) and who lived in a predominantly Christian culture (I understand Christian language and biblical allusions, but is it all true?).

So for three hundred years, Christians have, as incarnational servants, practiced an evangelism that focused on apologetics (presenting the gospel in a way that made rational sense) and addressed the gospel's impact on individuals (explaining what the gospel can do for an individual). Christians were also able to use insider Christian words and idioms, since Christian language was generally understood.

But then things began to change. In the early 1900s, the monolithic modern culture of the Enlightenment and its accompanying cultural assumptions began to diminish. The confidence and rational certainty that gave rise to the Age of Reason in the 1600s (think René Descartes) started to give way under the skepticism and existential doubt of the early 1900s (think Friedrich Nietzsche). Two World Wars, the dark side of colonialism and a technology-infused global mindset are among the many factors that have led to the gradual fading of the modern era and the emergence of a brand-new cultural landscape, which some are calling the postmodern era. In other words, things have indelibly changed in Western culture, and this has implications for how we do evangelism.

I grew up learning about evangelism from C. S. Lewis and Josh McDowell. The rational, logical arguments they armed me with (from Lord-Liar-Lunatic to "evidence that demands a verdict") were how I learned to be a witness. But I began running into people who just didn't itch where these tools scratched. For example, in Tacoma, Washington, I had an elderly coworker for a couple of years who was not a Christian. When our conversation one day got around to Christianity, she made it clear that she didn't believe Jesus ever existed. Let me clarify: it's not that she wasn't intellectually convinced of Jesus' divinity, she plain old didn't think he ever existed—at all. But she *was* convinced that we humans were brought to earth by aliens. And she wasn't a fringe oddball; she had a Ph.D. and was quite intelligent and well-read. In that conversation I found that all my well-practiced rational arguments lay limp before her odd combination of irrational incredulity (Jesus never existed) and random credulity (we come from aliens). At that point I started to wonder if my evangelism methods might not be fitted for this emerging, very different culture.

Later I met another non-Christian, Matthew, who was full of venom toward all things Christian. No questions, no intellectual inquiries—just venom. All my "evidence" seemed ill-fitted for someone so full of church-hurt, so distrustful of all things Christian. I found myself where many Missional Christians find themselves these days: equipped with evangelistic tendencies that aren't fitted for the age we live in.

Perhaps people in the West placed a strong emphasis on objective truth and human reasoning for three hundred years, but these days more and more people are placing a strong emphasis on

subjective human experience. And it isn't that they aren't interested in truth; they are quite interested in truth. They just ascribe
veracity differently. Rather than evaluating the truthfulness of the
gospel based on its logical sense, they want to know if it fits with
their experiences. This means the Missional Christian needs to be
good not only at apologetics, but also at telling stories—the story
of Scripture, the story of my own redemption, the story of God
working in me this week.

Perhaps people in the West thought in individualistic categories
for three hundred years, but these days more and more people are
thinking in communal, global categories. This doesn't mean
people aren't selfish (they still are); it's just that they think
in global categories. They want to know how the gospel helps this
world. Is it good news for this falling-apart, war-ridden, oppression-
littered world? This means the Missional Christian needs to understand not just how the gospel is good news for the individual
(for example, be able to draw the Bridge Diagram) but also how it
is good news for this world around us (for example, be able to
draw James Choung's Four Circles).

In this era of distrust for all things Christian, in a Western
culture where many people have dismissed Christianity out of
hand, the Missional Christian needs to learn how to build bridges
of trust and how to verbalize the gospel without using cliché
Christian words that many folks are allergic to and that, in our
post-Christian world, are nearly unintelligible.

Because God is still calling people to him (even in this in-
between, partly modern, partly postmodern, strange age we live
in) Missional Christians need to be willing, as servants, to retool
themselves for this age we are called to. I highly recommend that
Missional Christians sit under the teaching of culture watchers
and Christian leaders who have been watching these developments
in cultural change for some time. Laurence Singlehurst's *Sowing,
Reaping, Keeping: People-Sensitive Evangelism* is a great starting

place, and Lesslie Newbigin's profound but quite readable *Proper Confidence: Faith, Doubt, and Certainty in Christian Discipleship* provides incredible insights into the cultural shifts we are living through and must respond to thoughtfully.

5. *Coming to faith is a mysterious, organic journey.* When I first started thinking about evangelism, I was laboring under the assumption that becoming a Christian was a binary transaction: you're not a Christian, then you're a Christian. It's on or off. 1 or 0. And so I naturally concluded that evangelism was about helping (or forcing) someone to flip the switch. I had only one goal as a witness: get the switch flipped. Not only did this leave me often feeling like a failure (turns out switches don't flip every day), it also left me assuming that being a witness must be an aggressive activity. What else could cause someone's switch to flip before our conversation ended? This meant, in my case, that I often wound up saying nothing at all. (I liked my friends too much to pull out an aggressive Evangelism Shotgun and shoot it in their face.)

This was the case with my relationship with our new neighbor, Romie, in Boulder. When I first met Romie, she frightened me. She had come over to introduce herself and to let me know that I had put my recyclables in the recycling all wrong. Romie was a chain-smoking, free-spirited, retired schoolteacher. She was well-read and had a sharp wit and tongue, and she dropped hints early in our relationship that she was allergic to Christians. So I did what seemed the right thing to do: I tried to avoid bringing up the fact that I was a Christian. This witness-avoidance strategy wasn't just because of my fears and weakness (though those are well documented and were definitely in play), but because I was assuming that to be a witness with Romie meant shoving her across the line, saying something so inspiring and persuasive that her switch would flip. I occasionally contemplated dropping Lord-Liar-Lunatic into a conversation, but I knew she would shred it apart. So I said nothing.

At that time, I was beginning to be taught a profound truth:

conversion is a process. I began to understand that coming to faith isn't binary but is a mysterious, organic journey. I began to learn more about this journey and the different thresholds people cross on their way to Jesus. Each threshold is unique and carries with it different challenges, needs and questions. This has implications for those of us who are trying to introduce our friends to Jesus. I began to realize that before Romie (who was full of distrust for all things Christian) could actually consider the gospel, she needed to trust a Christian. This meant I didn't need to shove her across a line; I needed to be her friend. This realization has changed forever how I feel about relational evangelism, and it transformed my friendship with Romie.

Better understanding the mysterious yet organic conversion process allowed me to better empathize with Romie and serve her exactly where she was. When she needed to trust a Christian, I slowly helped engender trust and simply became a friend. When she needed to become curious about Jesus, I slowly helped pique her curiosity. When she needed to become open to change in her life, I modeled change in my own life. And on and on.

Though I started off scared of Romie, over time she became my best friend in Boulder. I talked with her more than any other friend; we shared holidays and joys and sadness together; we just sat and enjoyed each other's presence. And I was able to slowly and thoroughly share my faith with her in the warm light of our friendship.

That's the thing about relational evangelism. It's relational. And it's evangelism. When we moved from Boulder after eleven years (years rich in many profound relationships), I cried longest and hardest when I said goodbye to Romie. And she cried too. (And the two of us aren't really crying types.) I can't imagine I would have ever tasted the joys of our deep friendship had I continued to labor under the assumption that conversion is binary and evangelism aggressive. Understanding what it's like to journey to faith is empowering as a witness.

If you'd like to consider this conversion process from a theological perspective, I highly recommend reading Gordon T. Smith's *Beginning Well: Christian Conversion and Authentic Transformation.* For a practical, testimony-based look at how people come to faith these days and the implications for our witness, you might want to pick up the book Doug Schaupp and I cowrote, called *I Once Was Lost: What Postmodern Skeptics Taught Us About Their Path to Jesus.*

Serving the Lost

I've found that relational evangelism is perhaps the best-kept secret of the Christian life. On the one hand, it is calm, natural and pedestrian. On the other hand, it is eternal, crucial and life changing. Paul captured this reality well when writing to the Romans. On the one hand, the message of salvation is gorgeously profound, free and life changing: "everyone who calls on the name of the Lord will be saved" (Romans 10:13). Salvation is at stake, and all someone lost and mired in the darkness and decay of this world has to do is call on the name of Jesus. There is no better news than this. But Paul went on. "How then will they call on him in whom they have not believed? And how are they to believe in him of whom they have never heard?" (Romans 10:14). They have to hear before they can believe. Hearing and talking, words and conversation, sharing and storytelling—these are the everyday activities that carry the good news to those who need it. This means we fallible, imperfect believers get to be involved in the most profound human transformation possible, the most far-reaching rescue mission ever embarked on: we get to partner with God by carrying his good news.

The Missional Christian is honored to get to be a part of evangelism ("goodnewsing"). As Paul went on to marvel, "How beautiful are the feet of those who preach the good news!" (Romans 10:15). There's something attractive and sublime about serving the lost through relational evangelism. Jesus himself constantly initiated with the lost. He ate with them and had long, unhurried conversations with them. He was their friend—so much so that the religious people of his day felt uncomfortable with the company Jesus kept. One day they complained about this out loud, and so Jesus responded. He explained his relentless investment in the lost by telling three stories (see Luke 15).

The first was a story about a shepherd who lost a sheep. He left the ninety-nine other sheep to seek after that one lost sheep. The second story was about a woman who lost a coin. She tore her house apart until she found it. And the third story was about a father who went to great lengths to reconcile to himself his two lost sons. In other words, Jesus explained his own behavior (spending so much time with the lost) by pointing to God's profound heartbeat for those who are lost, God's relentless pursuit of them. Jesus was simply going about his father's business.

But Jesus had one more story to tell that day. He wanted his followers to know that they were supposed to follow suit. So in the parable of the shrewd manager (see Luke 16), Jesus invited his followers to use everything at their disposal to make friends with people in their social orbits who were lost. He was quite clear about the math: our purposefulness can lead to friendships that can lead to new people being saved for eternity. He urged his followers to be shrewd, thoughtful and purposeful in this endeavor because, as he lamented, "the people of this world are more shrewd in dealing with their own kind than are the people of the light" (Luke 16:8 NIV).

As I stand in my driveway and look around at my neighbors, I know that they are constantly being influenced by the "people of this world." So, as a person of the light, it is my honor to join God in his work of laboring shrewdly, thoughtfully and purposefully for the lost right here in my own social circles.

8

Thriving Church

To each is given the manifestation of the Spirit
for the common good.

1 CORINTHIANS 12:7

• • •

HERE I AM, standing in the lobby of my church. It's pretty clean in here, and most of the interior matches quite nicely. Our windows all have a "cathedral" shape to them, which is meant to echo the shape of the stained glass in the sanctuary. That stained glass is one of my favorite parts of the building: an artistically rendered Jesus with open arms. A rich light filters into the sanctuary through the glass, and when I sit in here, this church (founded in 1816) feels timeless. Of course, I also love Steffen Hall. That's where there are all sorts of lights set up and a stage area fit for dancing, acting, singing and rocking out to worship. They even have a laser machine somewhere up near the ceiling. This is my church. From the tidy classrooms to the memorial garden to the tiny chapel that has needlework scenes from the Bible—I love my church.

Of course, none of this is really the church. It's a building with walls and windows and gadgets and decorations. But this particular building is where my church meets. A community of believers gathers together here to pray, worship, confess, eat, read the Bible, study the Bible and talk about the Bible. Something is pulsing here in this building; something important is happening here. God's chosen tool, the local church, gathers here, is taught here and is equipped here.

This means God is at work here. Jesus was clear about this: "For where two or three are gathered in my name, there am I among them" (Matthew 18:20). God's local church (whether they are gathered in a steepled building or a home or a Starbucks) is a place God is at work. These are square inches that God is interested in.

The Need for Thriving Churches

While our culture may be quite taken with individual heroes, single protagonists and "lone rangers," God has always been much more taken with people—in the plural. From the time God called Abram and said, "I will make of you a great nation" (Genesis 12:2), God has called his people to be, well, a people. Plural. A community. The phrase "my people" is one of God's preferred ways of addressing us. From the time of Moses ("I will take you to be my people, and I will be your God," Exodus 6:7) to the time of the prophets ("So shall you be my people, and I will be your God," Jeremiah 11:4), God has been explicit about calling a people together.

From God's "nation" in the Old Testament to God's "church" in the New, God has made it clear that we are designed for community, we follow him in community, and we are sent out in community. The local church, then, is God's intended tool for our growth, our health and our ministry as his people. There is, of course, something a bit more sexy and exciting about events, books and new DVD series, but God's intention, his bread and butter, is to work through his faithful, confessing, worshiping, everyday church.

When God's church is thriving, his people are being fed. Worship, Word, sacraments, community—these are the meals that feed God's people, week in and week out. At the first Pentecost, when the Holy Spirit first came upon the church and three thousand people came to faith on the same day, we get this fascinating description of the life of the church: "And they devoted themselves to the apostles' teaching and the fellowship, to the breaking of bread and the prayers" (Acts 2:42). That pretty much covers it: the church comes together to handle God's Word, to be in real relationship with each other, to remember the cross as we take Communion, and to talk with God together in worship and prayer. When these things are in place, we grow as Christians.

And when God's church is thriving, his people are also being sent. As we've seen throughout this book, God not only saves and grows and nurtures Christians, he also invites us to get caught up with what he is doing in the world. In this way the church becomes an outpost of sorts, a launching pad for ministry and service to the world.

Our senior pastor, Tom Pfizenmaier, likes to think of our nearly two-hundred-year-old church as the House of Elrond. Fans of J. R. R. Tolkien's *The Hobbit* and the *Lord of the Rings* trilogy will be familiar with this "Last Homely House," an open home of respite securely nestled in Rivendell. It is a wide-open, hospitable, safe place for adventurers to rest, heal and sharpen their swords. This is where Frodo recovers and Bilbo writes, and where the fellowship of the ring is formed. The House of Elrond is a place of learning, mentoring and planning for the next mission. That's what our church is meant to be, Tom says. When God's church is thriving, his people are getting what they need to be used by him in this world.

In these ways, God's work is channeled through and anchored in thriving churches. This is God's design, and this has unavoidable implications for the Missional Christian.

The Role of the Missional Christian in the Church

If God is at work in and through the local church, Missional Christians will find themselves (at times) caught up in God's work in the church. In some contexts, it might be tempting to think that serving in the church is only the work of the ordained. God has called certain people, so the thinking goes, to "feed his sheep"— these are the pastors, priests, monks, ministers and nuns. The rest of us? We are the ones who go to church to be fed. Or so the thinking goes.

The reality is, God's church is not a bifurcated creature with two distinct parts. Rather, God's church is a single body, made up of many different members. Paul spoke of the church in this way: "For just as the body is one and has many members, and all the members of the body, though many, are one body, so it is with Christ" (1 Corinthians 12:12). He expanded the analogy, explaining that a body without varied and different parts wouldn't make any sense at all: "If the whole body were an eye, where would be the sense of hearing? If the whole body were an ear, where would be the sense of smell? But as it is, God arranged the members in the body, each one of them, as he chose. If all were a single member, where would the body be? As it is, there are many parts, yet one body" (vv. 17-20).

While it may be more common for us to conceive of the church as having two parts (the professionals who do the work and the normal Christians who sit in the pew), it is more biblical to conceive of the church as a body. Every Christian is a part of that body and has a role to play. The body doesn't work if only one or two parts are functioning. But when each part is doing its part, it is a beautiful thing to watch. It reminds you that God knew what he was doing when he formed the church.

For eleven years, Wendy and I were a part of a body called Hillside Church of the Savior. When we moved to Boulder, we knew we needed to join a church. (Individual Christians on their own are like floating body parts—they don't make sense.) We needed to find a body and attach ourselves to it. Hillside was that body. It was founded during the Jesus Movement and still had a definite hippie vibe: bluegrass worship, camping trips, worship songs from the seventies. But Hillside was unlike any church I had ever been a member of in a more significant way: there was no paid pastor or staff. Hillside had been carefully and diligently led by a rotating group of elders and deacons for years.

This stripped away all my assumptions about the work of the church being for "the professionals" as I watched computer programmers, moms, mechanics and meteorologists leading, serving, teaching and mentoring within the church. I was humbled to watch a very successful scientist take joy in setting up and taking down audiovisual equipment week after week. A businessman who held down two full-time jobs not only made the time to prepare brilliant sermons week after week, but also sat on the board of a missions-sending agency. Various people hosted prayer meetings and led Bible studies, planned retreats and followed up with visitors, visited the sick in the hospital and prayed with the hurting. And we all carried chairs.

For eleven years I saw firsthand what Paul was describing in 1 Corinthians: the body at work. Gone were my temptations to sit back and let the pros make sure the church was thriving. Instead, it was a joy to get caught up in God's work in the local church. First I took over the taping of sermons and making of tapes for folks who missed the service. Then I started playing guitar for worship. From time to time, I led the church service, prayed or shared a testimony before Communion. After several years I joined the "choir of preachers" who took turns standing up and teaching from God's Word.

I was becoming more missional right in my very own church. Not only was I being marked by God's work in the church, I was getting caught up in that same work. During those eleven years, I was a campus missionary; I went on two-month mission trips nearly every summer; and I was writing books and traveling around the country to speak. But God was also showing me what it meant to be missional right in my own local church. I was learning what Paul made clear right from the beginning: every Christian is a member of the body, which means they have a role to play in the local church.

There are a few things that are important to keep in mind as we seek to labor in our own churches.

Five Things to Keep in Mind While Serving Your Church

1. Servants meet needs. Before thinking about spiritual gifts and ministry "fit" (which are important to think about, as we shall see), it is first important to recognize that as servants we are sometimes called simply to meet felt needs. This is something a servant is more than willing to do: find a need and fill it.

Barnabas is a great example of such a servant in the early church. He was always willing to do what needed to be done. When the church needed money to care for the poor, Barnabas sold some property and donated the money to the church (see Acts 4). When newly converted Paul was turned away by the Jerusalem church leaders, Barnabas stepped forward and interceded for Paul, helping him reconcile with the those leaders (see Acts 9). When word reached Jerusalem that Hellenists were becoming Christians in Antioch, Barnabas agreed to make the trip north to find out what was happening (see Acts 11). When it turned out that there were many new believers who needed teaching and mentoring, Barnabas traveled to Tarsus to recruit Paul and then began teaching and mentoring with Paul in Antioch (see Acts 11). When the church in Antioch needed a collection for famine relief delivered to Jerusalem, Barnabas took it (see Acts 11). When God called him to be Paul's partner in mission, he went (see Acts 13).

When they needed someone to be an emissary to a theological counsel in Jerusalem, he went (see Acts 15).

If you are wondering where you are supposed to be serving in your church, it wouldn't hurt just to ask where there are needs. This is what I saw modeled beautifully at Hillside. If equipment, like a guitar or loud speaker, needed to be carried out to a car, all hands were willing to carry it. If we needed another leader for children's Sunday school, people stepped forward. I tell you, there's something about seeing a nationally recognized scientist or internationally recognized musician stack chairs that reminds you what servanthood is all about.

It is important to recognize, though, that there are unlimited unmet needs all around us, so we can't simply sign up for *every* need that we come across. I've seen this desire to say yes to every invitation chew people up and crush them. It's simply not sustainable or discerning, and it usually has at its roots some odd misunderstanding about our own abilities (as mini-Messiahs) or worth (I'm only worth something if I meet needs). This indiscriminate service also usually underestimates God's sovereignty and God's church (perhaps God is calling someone else to meet that need?).

So there needs to be a sense of balance: God is the one who determines our calling; needs do not. But simply stepping forward to serve where needed is often how we get caught up in God's work in our church. In high school, my Young Life leader, Ben Herr, asked me if I'd be willing to spend a month of my summer washing dishes at the camp where I became a Christian. At first it seemed an odd concept: spending my own money so I could wash dishes for a month? But after reading Charles Swindoll's *Improving Your Serve: The Art of Unselfish Living*, I realized what an absolute honor it would be to wash dishes for the sake of God's work in this world. And that's when it hit me: there must have been someone washing dishes the week *I* had been at the camp listening to the gospel message. I began wondering who was washing dishes that week and marveling at the fact that even washing dishes turns out to be an integral part of God's work in the world.

2. Every Christian has spiritual gifts. As Missional Christians take steps into serving in their local church, it is important for them to recognize that they have been specially empowered to serve and bless others. God gives spiritual gifts to his people to enable them to do the work he calls them to do. Missional Christians need to give some thought and attention to this very important topic, since God has given us gifts so that we might use them. Paul reminded the Corinthians, "Now concerning spiritual gifts, brothers, I do not want you to be uninformed" (1 Corinthians 12:1). So what do we need to know about spiritual gifts to be informed?

First, what are spiritual gifts? Spiritual gifts are given to the Christian by God. Paul wrote, "Now there are varieties of gifts, but the same Spirit; and there are varieties of service, but the same Lord; and there are varieties of activities, but it is the same God who empowers them all in everyone" (1 Corinthians 12:4-6). Paul never gave a comprehensive list of gifts, but the examples he gave in his letters give us a decent overview of some of the special empowerments God grants to his people:

- Administration
- Apostleship
- Discerning of spirits
- Evangelism
- Exhortation
- Faith
- Giving
- Healing
- Helps
- Interpretation of tongues

- Knowledge

- Leading

- Ministry

- Pastoring

- Prophecy

- Showing mercy

- Speaking in tongues

- Teaching

- Wisdom

- Working of miracles

Second, why are we given spiritual gifts? It is important to realize that God doesn't empower us so that we will be noticed and applauded. He empowers us for one simple reason. Paul put it this way: "To each is given the manifestation of the Spirit *for the common good*" (1 Corinthians 12:7, emphasis added). God empowers Christians so that they can bless others. It's a great irony that a gift meant to focus our labors on others can at times become such a source of introspective focus on ourselves. God doesn't give us spiritual gifts so that we can feel special or be recognized, but so that we can serve others.

Third, what are *my* spiritual gifts? This is actually a very important question to ask. If God has given you a gift, he intends you to use it. God had something in mind when he implanted spiritual gifts within you. Paul said of spiritual gifts that the Spirit "apportions to each one individually as he wills" (1 Corinthians 12:11). We don't get to choose our spiritual gifts; they are apportioned as God wills. So, how exactly do we discern what God has apportioned to us? Some suggest that you can take a simple survey to "figure out" your spiritual gifts. While such a survey might be helpful in your discernment process, it is highly unlikely that a simple test will help you discern your gifts. These tests often tell us more about our heroes (whose gifts we subconsciously admire and long to have) and our fears (which may make us averse to certain types of ministry, even though we might be meant for them).

True discernment happens over time, in community, in the course of serving. I've found that we don't discern our gifts before serving; rather, *in serving* we discern them. So it is wise and helpful to put our hands to a wide variety of service over the years. My advice: try everything. Be willing to try new things, even if they seem scary. In my own case, I've found that ministering in areas that I am weak (pastoring, prayer ministry, hospitality) has allowed God to shape me and grow me in ways I never would have if I had gone into a ministry where I solely used my gifts. For more thoughts on how God is "strong" in our "weakness," I highly recommend Marva Dawn's provocative *Powers, Weakness, and the Tabernacling of God*.

As we minister in various ways, discernment about our spiritual gifts comes when we begin to notice the kind of fruit that comes from our ministry and the kind of feedback that our community gives us. If you notice that a small amount of effort on your part produces a disproportionate amount of fruit, that might just mean something. And if multiple people say that a particular service of yours is very helpful, that might mean something too. Often we misdiagnose our own spiritual gifts, because when we are operating in our gifts, ministry "feels easy." That isn't a sign that it's not a gift: it might be a sign that it *is* a gift. If you want to explore this fascinating and important topic more, you might want to work your way through the LifeGuide Bible Study *Spiritual Gifts* by Paul Stevens.

3. Leadership is essential. God has purposefully imbedded leadership within his church. The specific form of this leadership has had many different names and iterations over the years (from elders and deacons in the early centuries to ordained priests and pastors to small-group leaders to staff to worship leaders to Sunday School teachers to . . . well, many of the leadership roles you probably see in your own church). While the style of leadership varies from church to church and the formality of leadership does as well, the one common denominator is that God's church needs leadership. This means two very important things for every church: (1) people need to submit to their leaders, and (2) people need to be willing to lead when called upon.

For me, the first truth came more easily. I had wonderful leaders as a young Christian and took joy in submitting to their leadership, praying for them and following their lead. This set me up to trust future church leaders implicitly, and I found myself automatically wanting them to succeed. From Ben to Troy to Larry to Sue . . . all down the years I have been blessed with godly leaders from the time I became a Christian.

I recognize that some Christians have had a very different experience. I've had friends who were hurt by leaders in the past and so carried with them an instinctual distrust toward every other church leader. Their arms were always crossed (whether in reality or just metaphorically) as they kept themselves from allowing their leaders to come close or influence them. Unfortunately this negative attitude has a way of spreading, like a nasty cold, to those around them, and they wind up undermining their leaders (whether intentionally or not). Others have a hard time submitting to leadership because of their pride, their own lust for power or just a general spirit of rebellion. Whether reticent to submit because of hurt or fear or sin, it is possible for every Christian to heal and grow and learn the joys of submission.

For me, the second truth (people need to be willing to lead) was the harder one to learn. Ben invited me to share a devotion at a Young Life retreat in high school, and I found myself sweating over the preparations. I found my pride itching as I was tempted to lead a devotion that would make others think well of me. I found myself jealous as others freely played all afternoon while I spent time thinking about the devotion. On top of that, I just plain wasn't interested in being a leader. I didn't feel like a leader; I didn't feel worthy to lead; and the temptations that came with leadership sealed the deal for me: I wasn't going to lead.

Except there's this whole thing about leadership being essential in God's church. And as I got more and more caught up in God's work, I found myself agreeing to more and more leadership roles: from leading a Bible study to leading a worship service to leading a mission trip. And over the years I have learned to embrace and enjoy this central part of God's work in his church. There are hundreds of great leadership books that one could read to learn more. The first one that helped me embrace my own place as a leader was Henri Nouwen's elegant and understated *In the Name of Jesus: Reflections on Christian Leadership.* Especially if you don't see yourself as a typical leader, this might be a helpful read.

Many of my friends have taken to leadership with much more grace than I have. They haven't aggressively pushed for leadership roles because of pride, they haven't shrugged and tried to avoid leadership roles—rather, they have simply said yes when invited to lead. And this is part of what makes God's church thrive: God's people helping lead his church. Thankfully the Bible is full of models of godly leadership for us to learn from—chief among them Jesus himself. Some of Jesus' patterns as a leader have been thoughtfully expounded by Leighton Ford in his book *Transforming Leadership: Jesus' Way of Creating Vision, Shaping Values and Empowering Change.* The church thrives when it is led by servant leaders who follow after Jesus.

4. No one is meant to be an island. As we have seen, our lives as Christians are meant to be lived together with others. This is what God intended when calling a "people" to himself. This is the "fellowship" that the early Christians devoted themselves to. There is a richness and joy and abundance that comes from living as we are intended in community. As Psalm 133 puts it in picture form:

> Behold, how good and pleasant it is when brothers dwell in unity! It is like the precious oil on the head, running down on the beard, on the beard of Aaron, running down on the collar of his robes! It is like the dew of Hermon, which falls on the mountains of Zion! For there the Lord has commanded the blessing, life forevermore. (vv. 1-3)

Oil on the beard and morning dew may not seem so special to us, but these are luxurious images of plenty—a fitting image for what comes from the blessings of community.

I am fascinated with language, and I find it interesting that "family" language caught on so quickly among the earliest Christians. Right away Christians started calling each other "brother," "mother," "sister." We may be used to hugging a friend at church and saying, "My brother from another mother!" but this phenomenon of family language was brand-new in the church. And it is a sign, I think, of the richness of Christian community. As someone who grew up as something of a loner (longing for the day when I could move to that cabin in the woods and finally be alone), I was at first fearful of, and eventually utterly thankful for, Christian community. Dietrich Bonhoeffer's *Life Together* is a fascinating view of what's really possible in Christian community and is right up there with my favorite practical look at how community and growth are intertwined: Jean Vanier's *Community and Growth*.

But not only is life as a Christian meant to be lived together with others, our ministry and service is likewise meant to be done in partnership with other Christians. We're not meant to labor alone. When Jesus sent his disciples out into ministry, he always sent them together—at the very least in pairs. And while we may focus on Paul as a singular man of mission, he too was always sent out with others: Barnabas, Titus, Silas, Timothy. In the church, plurality has always been intentional and explicit. There is a reason that plurality in leadership is the norm in the Bible and that "ministry teams" are the norm in many of our churches today.

I have experienced firsthand why we are meant to always have plurality in leadership and ministry in teams. When I became an InterVarsity area director, I threw myself into the role with all my energy, gifts and abilities . . . and found out a mere two months later that this was not enough. And never would be. A couple of months in, I was writing in a journal, processing the mistakes I had made, misjudgments I had arrived at, details I had missed, and I found myself drawing a picture of a head with a huge hole on one side. *That's me,* I thought, as I looked at the drawing. I have blind spots and limitations.

As I began to labor collaboratively with those around me (with Megan, Ryan and Dulcy), I discovered that we're all like that little drawing: we're all gifted in some ways and not in others. I lacked good shepherding instincts for the women in our group, but Megan was fabulous at that. Ryan was incredible at handling large groups of people in stressful situations, which was exactly what I needed to help me lead our urban mission. And Dulcy's huge spiritual radar was a God-send in meetings where I always seemed to focus in on the content of what we were deciding, not on how the people in the room were doing. We are all uniquely gifted and limited, which is why we are meant to lead and serve together with others.

5. *You can bring a couple of others along with you.* When I first became a Christian, my Young Life leader, Ben, was like a big brother to me. He encouraged me, let me ask questions, studied the Bible with me and came to see some of my tennis matches. I looked up to him and felt lucky that he wanted to spend time with me. When I got to college, Troy Anderson, a senior living in my dorm, led the Bible study that I attended, and he began meeting with me, encouraging me and helping me ask my questions and

continue to grow. We would go for long walks around campus or play basketball together. I felt blessed that God had given me another older brother to mentor me. My sophomore year, I met Larry, another Christian, who likewise came to be something of an older brother to me. I was soaking in the richness of one of the basic elements of Christian community: discipleship. Or mentoring. Or spiritual friendship. Whatever you call it, it is central to a thriving community: believers helping each other follow God.

This is the kind of relationship Timothy seems to have had with Paul. In Acts 16 Luke tells us a bit about their meeting, and throughout Acts and Paul's letters, we get glimpses into the spiritual friendship they had. Timothy became something of a protégé of Paul's, but their relationship wasn't just about ministry training: it was intimate and dealt with matters of the heart and character as well. Second Timothy is an amazing window into this Paul-Timothy relationship: Paul is near his death and is writing a last letter to "Timothy, my beloved child" (2 Timothy 1:2). Paul's letter helps us see that his mentorship of Timothy has been marked by love and labor:

> I thank God whom I serve, as did my ancestors, with a clear conscience, as I remember you constantly in my prayers night and day. As I remember your tears, I long to see you, that I may be filled with joy. I am reminded of your sincere faith, a faith that dwelt first in your grandmother Lois and your mother Eunice and now, I am sure, dwells in you as well. For this reason I remind you to fan into flame the gift of God, which is in you through the laying on of my hands, for God gave us a spirit not of fear but of power and love and self-control. (2 Timothy 1:3-7)

Even this short section shows us that Paul knows Timothy well, prays for him, loves him, seems to know some of his weaknesses and calls him to grow. It's this kind of Paul-Timothy relationship that has allowed the church to flourish down through the years. In fact, one of Paul's reasons for writing to Timothy was to encourage him to mentor other Christians in the same way Paul had mentored him: "You then, my child, be strengthened by the grace that is in Christ Jesus, and what you have heard from me in the presence of many witnesses entrust to faithful men who will be able to teach others also" (2 Timothy 2:1-2).

Paul is basically saying, what I've done for you, you now go and do for others. This is the exact conversation Larry had with me one day while walking on a beach in Oregon together. We had been walking along, talking about life and the Bible and Jesus (as we often did) when Larry said, "What do you think about Loo?" I wasn't sure what he meant. Lewis (Loo) was a new freshman on campus; he was a friend and a young Christian. Quite similar to Paul's encouragement to Timothy, Larry invited me to do for Loo what Larry and Troy had done for me.

To be honest, I was perplexed. I had always seen myself as the younger brother. I told Larry that someone else, someone more mature, should come alongside Loo. But Larry just smiled and asked me to pray about it. And I did. And later that day I asked Loo if he wanted to go for a walk on the beach. Loo shrugged and said, "Sure." And thus began another spiritual friendship.

I still remember the look on Loo's face a year or so later when I invited him to initiate a mentor relationship with a new freshman on campus. Thus the faith gets encouraged in Christians generation after generation. And thus the church thrives. I had been mentored well by Ben, Troy and Larry, so I had a model to follow when befriending Loo. But I recognize that not everyone has such a luxury. This is why I find Rich Lamb's practical look at community among Christians so helpful. *The Pursuit of God in the Company of Friends* has some great chapters on how to help encourage others in their faith, whether your "mentoring" of them is formal or informal. By far the most influential book I've ever read about this element of the Christian life is *The Master Plan of Evangelism* by Robert Coleman. I must have read that one ten times by now. Ideally we will each have a "Paul" and a "Timothy" in our life as Christians. That's how it's supposed to work.

Serving Your Church

If you were to visit the building my church meets in, you might be struck and impressed, as I first was, by the profound three-panel stained-glass windows depicting Jesus with open arms. But what's more profound and more beautiful, by far, is the community of Christians who are based here: ordinary, everyday folks who come through these doors to pray and chat and worship and laugh and then go out of these doors to meet in small groups and share the good news and serve others and gather around kitchen tables. The Holy Spirit abides within these people, and God chooses to work in and through them.

God's greatest gifts to us are often each other. But it's a funny thing about people: there's not a perfect one among us. Maybe it's just my church, but everyone here is like me: a sinner who's being redeemed. This means that, over time, we hurt each other and have conflicts. We apologize and forgive. At times the messiness of real people becomes bothersome to some. Some of us feel embarrassed and unworthy when our own sins show through a bit. And it can be tempting when faced with our own lack and limitations to withdraw, to pull back from those around us and forsake community.

But, as Paul reminds us, that's not how it's supposed to be with a body. He wrote, "If the foot should say, 'Because I am not a hand, I do not belong to the body,' that would not make it any less a part of the body. And if the ear should say, 'Because I am not an eye, I do not belong to the body,' that would not make it any less a part of the body" (1 Corinthians 12:15-16). We need to remember—no matter how lacking we may feel, no matter how messy our own mess—that we are a part of God's church. We are meant to live, warts and all, in community.

At other times we can grow weary and frustrated with other people when their sins and limitations start showing through. It can be tempting in those times to want these messy people to just leave. But, as Paul reminds us, that's not how it's supposed to be with a body either:

The eye cannot say to the hand, "I have no need of you," nor again the head to the feet, "I have no need of you." On the contrary, the parts of the body that seem to be weaker are indispensable, and on those parts of the body that we think less honorable we bestow the greater honor, and our unpresentable parts are treated with greater modesty, which our more presentable parts do not require. But God has so composed the body, giving greater honor to the part that lacked it, that there may be no division in the body, but that the members may have the same care for one another. If one member suffers, all suffer together; if one member is honored, all rejoice together. (1 Corinthians 12:21-26)

We need to remember—no matter how messy other folks' messes—that we are all God's church. We are meant to live, warts and all, in community.

Where does this leave us? As messy people living into the rich gift of community, as Missional Christians who are caught up in God's work not only outside our church walls, but within them as well. This isn't something we get perfect, but it is something we need to commit ourselves to. As the author of Hebrews summed it all up so well, "And let us consider how to stir up one another to love and good works, not neglecting to meet together, as is the habit of some, but encouraging one another, and all the more as you see the Day drawing near" (Hebrews 10:24-25).

9

Urban Mercy

Seek the welfare of the city.

JEREMIAH 29:7

• • •

WHEN I DRIVE twenty minutes away from my neighborhood, my car enters another world. Twenty short minutes is not so far away geographically, but it can seem like a world away culturally. My own neighborhood (this Judea of mine) is culturally familiar to me; the sights and sounds and rhythms make sense to me. I know people here, and people know me. But only twenty minutes away from my house lies a very different place—the city of St. Louis.

Just as Jesus asked his disciples to step across the cultural boundary that separated Judea and Samaria, so God calls each of us (at some point) to cross our own nearby cultural barriers (wherever they may be) and get caught up in God's work among those who are different from us. In my own world, this means getting caught up in God's work in the city.

Jesus' disciples were unsure about Samaria. They had been taught their whole lives to avoid Samaria, and so even the idea of stepping into Samaria made their missional feet shake in their missional boots. (The disciples once asked Jesus if they could call flame balls from heaven down on a Samaritan village.) And we're not so different today. (The Safe Christian locks his car doors when driving through the city, for example.) When it comes to the city, a lifetime of clichés, stereotypes, prejudice and well-meant warnings can combine with our own hesitance to make us a bit queasy about God's work in the city.

Some things never change—including our leeriness of places that are different, and God's passionate interest in every square inch, including the city.

The Need for Urban Mercy

There was a time, a few decades ago, when alert Christians began to notice the global population shift toward urban centers. Poorer countries were leading the way; the poor, desperate for a job, began streaming into megacities like Calcutta, Mexico City and Sao Paulo. But the rest of the world was not far behind; for a variety of interrelated reasons our world's population was moving into the city. Christians began speaking, wisely and rightly, of the "new mission field" that our cities represented.

This was a few decades ago. Now, perhaps, it is more fitting to speak of the city as the inevitable, obvious mission field. Cities everywhere are growing, representing more square inches of this world than ever before. In fact, if you are looking at where the people are, cities are disproportionately important and strategic square inches for God's people to minister in.

The city is a mission field of unique needs and opportunities. The needs are somewhat obvious: underfunded schools, decaying older buildings, homelessness, poverty, unemployment, racial tension. The opportunities are nearly astounding: large numbers of people in a small area, a steady influx of refugees and immigrants from all around the world, a diverse and creative church. The city is a vibrant area that God is actively at work within.

There's nothing new about this. God has always been interested in the city. From the time Adam, Eve, Cain and Abel stumbled out of the garden and formed cities, God has followed his people there. God had his own people establish cities of safe-haven, and his redemptive work within cities is found throughout the Bible. Not only did God's people build Jerusalem, but God used this as an image of the perfect consummation of his kingdom, when the New Jerusalem will come down from heaven. Our eternity, it turns out, will not be spent in isolated, rural getaways, but in a city—the City of God.

Cities were strategically important to the early church as the gospel was spread from urban center to urban center (Jerusalem, Antioch, Ephesus, Athens, Rome) and then from there to the surrounding countryside. And God's passionate interest in the poor, the widows, the travelers and the down-and-out obviously has implications in a world where cities act as collecting grounds for such people.

So the city has always been an important mission field in many ways. There is great need and opportunity in the city, and so it's no surprise that God can be found right at the heart of the city, dispensing his loving mercy on the people there. The city has been, and continues to be, an important part of God's work in this world. This has unavoidable implications for the Missional Christian.

The Role of the Missional Christian in the City

From Paul and Peter in first-century Palestine and Asia Minor, to Pope Gregory in sixth-century Rome, to William Booth in nineteenth-century London, to Mother Teresa in twentieth-century Calcutta, God's people have been getting caught up in God's work in the city. But it's not just apostles, popes and saints who are called to such work—everywhere God's at work in a city, you find his missional people getting caught up in that work.

After my freshman year of college, I was invited to spend two weeks living and learning on "the other side" of Tacoma. My university was nestled among upper-middle-class homes on one side of Tacoma, but this Tacoma Urban Project was over on the other side of Tacoma. (The side I had been told wasn't safe.) We moved into a couple of dingy apartments, and I began to see firsthand what Paul, Gregory and Booth had seen: the pulsing, vibrant work of God in the city and what it's like to get caught up in urban ministry. As it turns out, urban ministry isn't about a one-off spasm of volunteerism; it's about being a Missional Christian—eyes, hands, feet, heart and soul—in the midst of the city.

With Sober Eyes, the Missional Christian is willing to look beyond the stereotypes and the graffiti to learn what's really going on in the city. Sober Eyes can't see much from the freeway, so Missional Christians slow down and drive roads they've never seen before, read the newspaper more carefully and listen to the stories of those who live in the city. Rather than vaguely sighing at the stereotyped problems of the city, Missional Christians dig deeper, get to know real people and find out—in detail—about the darkness and decay within the city.

Then they put their Servant Hands to use. Missional Christians don't come to the city primarily to lead and teach and save the day, but to serve—to put their hands to use tending to the needs of others, washing feet that may be dirtier than the feet they're used to handling. They do this even if the service takes them into parts of town they've never seen before, parts of town they've heard about and been told to avoid at all costs, parts of town where they are perhaps for the first time in the minority. They step forward with Ready Feet, willing to follow God wherever he is at work.

God is vibrantly, relentlessly at work in the city. And as Missional Christians get caught up in God's work in the city, it affects their Compassionate Hearts, causes pain and induces crying as they enter into the suffering of others. As the testimony of countless Christians shows us, laboring alongside God in the city does something to your very soul—making you cling to God, changing you, ushering you into a kind of solid joy that simply parachuting into the city for concerts and games can never provide.

As you follow God into the city in search of that joy, there are some very important things to keep in mind.

Five Things to Keep in Mind While Serving in the City

1. *You should enter the city with humility and grace.* It is a common temptation for those of us going into the city for the sake of God's work there to bring with us a subtle posture of arrogance and accusation. We ride in on white horses, sure that we can save the day. And we wrinkle our noses at how "wrong" things are done in the city. But it turns out that arrogance and accusation are not great entry postures. Instead, we ought to enter the city with humility and grace, ready to learn and be taught as much as we are going to teach.

One summer, some friends and I moved into East Palo Alto, California, to help run a summer-long tutoring program. You may have heard of Palo Alto—home of Stanford University and pristine suburban neighborhoods. We were moving into East Palo Alto, which is just on the other side of the freeway—and a world away. When we first toured EPA, I was stunned by the sight of a burned-out car on the side of a road (Is this a war zone?) and silenced by the sight of the abandoned high school that was being used as a food pantry (Does no one else get the irony of this?). I felt slightly scared, and—I have to admit as I look back—fairly arrogant.

Halfway through the summer, I was running up against my limitations and my lack of understanding. I was beginning to realize that maybe the kids of EPA had a lot more to teach me than I had thought. This humbling shift was cemented one afternoon when a policeman pulled me over on my route back from the tutoring center. I was driving our minivan and was pretty sure I had stopped at that last stop sign, but when the policeman asked me to step out of the car, I began to wonder and when he asked me to turn around and face the van, I figured I was in for my first-ever pat-down. But at that point the policeman simply pointed to the top of the van—where there was a big box of popsicles. I had put them up there while loading the van and had driven off with the box still up there. I blushed as the policeman said, "Those yours?"

"Yes."

"What are you doing with popsicles in EPA?"

"I came here to run a tutoring program, to teach the kids," I responded.

The policeman looked at me, looked up at the box and shrugged, shaking his head. "Who's teaching who?" he said. And with that he walked away.

I was embarrassed. I wanted to call out and correct his grammar (it should be "Who's teaching *whom*") but I got my box of melting popsicles, got back in the van and faced the beautiful truth: I had a lot to learn. It's this posture of humility and grace that is needed whenever you step into a new culture for the sake of ministry. We step in as learners, recognizing our limits. We look around us, not to criticize and shake our heads, but to look for partners and lessons.

While it may seem most natural to couch our service in the city in terms of *service* (I am going to the city to serve), it is just as appropriate to say that we go to work in the city to learn (I am going to the city to be changed). For more on this critical entry posture, read Robert Lupton's *Theirs Is the Kingdom: Celebrating the Gospel in Urban America*. It's a quick read, and I wouldn't recommend putting your hand to urban ministry without getting to know this well-written, humble classic.

2. *You need partners in the city.* Whenever those from outside the city feel called to minister inside the city, they need to find partners. Crosscultural ministry—even if it's taking place only

twenty minutes from your driveway—is complex and tricky. True crosscultural partners are a gift from God; they help us learn, understand and minister in more effective, communal ways. Crosscultural ministry without a partner inside the culture is a recipe for disaster. So it is always worth the time and energy it takes to find a good partner.

In 1999 I started to look for a partner in Denver. My family and a dozen college students from nearby Boulder were looking to spend the summer of 2000 in the inner city of Denver, and I was sent to seek out a partner for our time there. Elias and I hit it off from the beginning. He was a missionary from Chile who had come to the United States to minister in Sun Valley, an historically challenged neighborhood ringed by highways just a stone's throw from the Denver Broncos' Mile High Stadium. Elias was pastor of the only church inside Sun Valley and was interested in meeting to hear what I was thinking.

We had lunch at a nearby Mexican restaurant, and halfway through the lunch I felt that we had found our partner. All that was left was hammering out the details, I figured, as I ordered a second "Mexican Coke" at the counter.

But Elias kept asking me questions: What did I mean when I said "partnership"? Who would be deciding what ministry we would pursue in Sun Valley? How would we determine the schedule? What kind of training would the students get before setting foot in Sun Valley? Were we just interested in the summer and nothing else? His questions set me back on my heels a bit. Had I done something to lose his trust? Was this some Chilean attention to detail I wasn't used to?

After our *third* meeting to discuss a *potential* partnership, it was clear to me: as a minister in the city, he was constantly being approached by well-meaning suburban churches and Christian groups wanting to "do some good in the city." But many of them weren't really interested in a partnership or in Elias or even in the city. Mostly they were interested in doing their good deed—as quickly and as cheaply as possible. Elias had seen the rich "use" the poor to scratch their own philanthropic itches, and thus the many questions.

A crosscultural partnership is not quick or easy or painless to develop. But it is essential. Elias and I enjoyed an intense four-year relationship with our families living together for two of the summers. In that time Elias and I learned from each other, confessed to each other, forgave each other. We made decisions together, shared leadership and evaluated our partnership regularly. Our groups from outside the city couldn't have done it alone. For more on this exciting dance of finding a partner and nurturing a healthy partnership in the city, peruse *Linking Arms, Linking Lives: How Urban-Suburban Partnerships Can Transform Communities* written by a community of wise statesmen of urban ministry, Ronald J. Sider, John M. Perkins, Wayne L. Gordon and F. Albert Tizon.

3. People are what replace stereotypes. "I'm scared to walk downtown; the youth in the city are just so . . . " "White folks just don't get it; they are always thinking about . . . " "Homeless people make me so mad; they need to . . . " Any time you cross cultures, you are inevitably bringing with you stereotypes about those who are different from you. Jesus' disciples hated Samaritans and undoubtedly knew all sorts of "Samaritan jokes." It took the explicit modeling of Jesus and the encouragement of the Holy Spirit to make them even step into Samaria. It took the reconciling power of the gospel to overcome a lifetime of stereotypes, making it possible for Paul to proclaim "Here there is not Greek and Jew, circumcised and uncircumcised, barbarian, Scythian, slave, free; but Christ is all, and in all" (Colossians 3:11).

The bad news is, we all carry stereotypes and caricatures of others around with us. We're all a bit racist and classist. The good news is, stereotypes have a way of quickly melting away under the warm heat of friendship. I knew a group of Christian students from Montana who made an annual road trip through the Rockies. Their trip inevitably took them straight through Denver, which made a few of them quite nervous. Denver was a big place compared to Bozeman, Montana. You didn't run into many homeless men or street kids in Bozeman. So everything this group of Christians "knew" about the homeless and street kids was based purely on stereotypes (many of them from movies), and this "knowledge" made them nervous whenever they drove through Denver.

But several of these students decided to move to Denver for a summer as part of one of our Denver Urban Partnerships. They moved right into the city and partnered with Scum of the Earth Church, a creative inner-city church that had its fair share of homeless folks and street kids. And one interaction at a time, they began to meet "the homeless." While hanging out at Sox Place (a drop-in center for homeless kids), while skateboarding downtown, while serving food before Scum's worship services, they met real people. They shook hands and laughed at jokes and shot the breeze. They heard stories and told their own. In this way their stereotypes were replaced with relationships. Not only were they no longer afraid of Denver, a few folks from that team wound up moving there and have been ministering among the homeless ever since. (If you're curious, Pastor Mike Sares has written a book about Scum called *Pure Scum: The Left-Out, the Right-Brained and the Grace of God*.)

Crosscultural ministry forced the early church to confront its stereotypes and bigotries, and it forces us to do the same. Rigorous self-examination and humble honesty in this area is important for all of us. Rule of thumb: if you ever find yourself claiming something about "those people," stop and ask yourself if you can name at least three of "those people." If you can't, you probably need to withdraw your statement and maybe think about taking a road trip of your own—even if it is to a place only twenty minutes away.

For more on this beautiful process, you might want to give *More than Equals: Racial Healing for the Sake of the Gospel* by Spencer Perkins and Chris Rice an honest read. In my own process as a white man, I've also found the book *Being White: Finding Our Place in a Multiethnic World* by Paula Harris and Doug Schaupp to be very helpful.

4. You can have mercy on individuals. Whenever ministering crossculturally, it is inevitable that we feel out of place and unsure of what to do from time to time. You stand in line at the soup kitchen dispensing food, not sure if you should make eye contact with the guests or not. Someone comes up to you asking for spare change, and you hesitate. *(Am I supposed to be generous and give to everyone who asks of me . . . or does this actually hurt them in the long run if I give?)* These unsure moments are natural—learning is like that. And learning how to minister in the city takes time. But as you take tentative steps into urban ministry, there is one task that you can always engage in: having mercy on someone standing near you.

Steve had been going to St. Louis Cardinals games with his son Brendan for years. And he had been asked for money many times while down near Busch Stadium for games. But one Sunday night a few years back, after the Cards won, something was different. Steve had heard a sermon on Matthew 25 earlier that morning ("as you did it to one of the least of these my brothers, you did it to me," v. 40). As Steve walked right past a man asking for change, he couldn't shake the words from Scripture. But he wasn't sure what the right thing to do was. He knew little about "the homeless" in St. Louis, and he wasn't a crosscultural expert. But Steve felt nudged by God to have mercy on this man standing in front of him.

So Steve handed the man two dollars. A simple act. It didn't take a lot of time, but it was tangible and practical. It was a simple act of mercy. That one experience made Steve wonder more about what it was like to be homeless and the difference a simple gift of food could make. So he began looking for partners in the city and wound up in an ongoing relationship with The Bridge Homeless Ministry in downtown St. Louis.

Steve is a member of my church, Bonhomme, in the suburbs of St. Louis and has now recruited several families to join him regularly in serving food to the homeless at The Bridge. Simple acts of mercy, one week at a time. Once a year Steve and others at Bonhomme coordinate a large steak-dinner cookout. Dozens of people from Bonhomme donate steaks, burgers, hot dogs and ice cream, and head down to The Bridge to have a huge party. These folks from the suburbs aren't experts in caring for the homeless (the folks at The Bridge are). Rather, they are doing something solid and practical: having mercy on individuals. Whether we are offering a listening ear, a smile, a piggy-back ride, a simple meal or a moment of our time, we can have mercy on someone standing near us. This is part of what it means to be missional in the city.

5. You can pursue systemic change and renewal. The image is a bit simplistic and clichéd by overuse, but it illustrates an important lesson: A group is visiting a river and is shocked when they see a baby being washed away in its current. They immediately form a human chain and pull the baby from the river. But they notice there are more babies in the river. So they throw themselves heroically into rescuing babies from the river. This goes on for some time until one woman separates from the group and starts walking upstream. "What are you doing?" her friends yell at her. She doesn't stop walking but calls back over her shoulder, "I'm going to go see who's throwing babies in the river!" While we can always throw ourselves into having mercy on individuals, God sometimes may call us to "walk upstream" and pursue systemic change.

Becka was a part of our first summer-long adventure in Denver. She was there when we invited that first group of students to join us in partnering with Elias in Sun Valley. She was there when we crowded into a hot, old Sunday school room to do training on how to cross cultures with grace and humility. She leaned over her Bible as we sat on folding chairs studying about God's heart for the poor. She was there when we started tutoring energetic, sometimes-challenging children in the Sun Valley Youth Center, having mercy on the kids in her group. Becka was doing everything I expected: learning from Elias and others, having her worldview challenged, having mercy on the neighborhood kids. But then one night she did something I didn't expect.

We were just finishing a Bible study on Amos. We were gathered around a cheap folding table in the church offices and had just considered God's anger at injustice and the call for his people to do away with injustice. This Bible study, followed by some basic statistics about injustice in the city, left everyone mourning the plight of the city. This I expected and, frankly, hoped for. But then Becka (normally the quiet one) slammed her hands down on the table, looked over at me and said, "So, who do we call?"

I wasn't sure what she was talking about. She went on: "Who do we call? Is there a city office we can call? They need to know there's injustice in their city. We need to do something about this." My instinct was to endure Becka's naiveté, but then I realized she was asking a really good question. It's one thing—a quite beautiful and important thing—to have mercy on individuals; it's quite another to pursue systemic change and renewal. Becka wanted to walk upstream and see who was throwing babies in the water. And her instincts are thoroughly biblical.

God cries out against injustice and calls his people to pursue justice. This could involve everything from empowering the oppressed to questioning biased systems to confronting unjust policies and laws. As we minister in the city, this is something we eventually find ourselves pondering. Kevin Blue's *Practical Justice: Living Off-Center in a Self-Centered World* is a good place to start searching for answers. Blue is a deep Christian who writes from years of experience in the city. His helpful book is theologically grounded and consummately practical.

Serving in the City

Just as Jeremiah called the exiles to "seek the welfare" of the city they were sent to, many Christians are also called to find out about and get caught up in God's work in cities today. For those of us who are not from the city, this call may go against some of our deeper instincts. Safe, Successful and Happy Christians find little reason to get involved in God's work there. For those of us who are from the city, this call may go against our instincts as well: the pains and messes of urban life and ministry are enough to tempt us to abandon the city.

We see this temptation expressed well in Psalm 55. The psalmist has seen the city with Sober Eyes: "For I see violence and strife in the city. Day and night they go around it on its walls, and iniquity and trouble are within it; ruin is in its midst; oppression and fraud do not depart from its marketplace" (vv. 9-11). And his temptation is to flee from the city: "Oh, that I had wings like a dove! I would

For a helpful guide on tending to your own growth as you labor in the city, check out Randy White's *Encounter God in the City: On-Ramps to Personal and Community Transformation*. For an in-depth theology of God and the city, sit yourself under the teaching of Manuel Ortiz and Harvie Conn, whose comprehensive book *Urban Ministry: The Kingdom, the City and the People of God* serves almost as a graduate course in urban theology. If you are considering relocating to the city for good, you might want to read Randy White's *Journey to the Center of the City: Making a Difference in an Urban Neighborhood* or Robert Lupton's *Renewing the City*.

fly away and be at rest; yes, I would wander far away; I would lodge in the wilderness" (vv. 6-7).

Ah, *the wilderness*. The bucolic rural life. The calm suburban life. And yet . . . And yet . . . God is also at work in the city. This has implications for the Missional Christian who is caught up in God's work in this world—even if it happens to be in the city. Does the psalmist run away from the city? In the end, no. Instead, he calls out to God for help. "But I call to God, and the Lord will save me" (v. 16). And the psalmist encourages others to do the same: "Cast your burden on the Lord, and he will sustain you" (v 22).

Serving with God in the city causes the Missional Christian to cry out to God in this same way. It is something of a paradox that some of the most painful, confusing moments of my life have been while engaged with God's work and God's people in the city, and yet some of the most beautiful, exhilarating moments of my life have been in the exact same place. Always my relationship with God seems dialed up while serving in the city.

When the Missional Christian goes and joins God in the city, it causes her to grow and be changed. It provides precious glimpses of redemptive work so heartbreakingly beautiful, so humble and powerful, that we are left forever changed. It brings blessed cross-cultural relationships with mature Christians living in the city. Serving in the city teaches us more about ourselves, our God and the city. Sometimes the Missional Christian needs to follow the advice of the psalmist and not sprout wings and fly away from the city, but rather pray to God from the heart of the city he so loves.

10

Global Partnerships

For so the Lord has commanded us, saying, "I have made you a light for the Gentiles, that you may bring salvation to the ends of the earth."

ACTS 13:47

● ● ●

I'M SITTING ON A PLANE, and God's world is spinning beneath me. It's all a bit dizzying. I was standing on my driveway just a few hours ago, but now I'm way up here. I have a window seat, so I can look down at God's world, so small-looking from up here, and get thoughtful.

"You will be my witnesses in Jerusalem, Judea, Samaria . . . and to the ends of the earth." That's what Jesus said to his disciples. And my heart moves within me at the sound of that last phrase—*the ends of the earth*. The ends of the earth? Those provincial Galileans—why send them way over there? How mind bending and nearly unbelievable must that have been for those small-town men?

And me? Hamburger-loving, English-speaking, bug-not-liking, ethnocentric, current-events-and-geography-ignorant me? The ends of the earth *and me*? Here the mental ruts are almost too deep to overcome. Khaki-wearing-brave-knight-missionary types go over there. Don't they? Them There Then: that's the world-missions cadence I'm used to. But me? My heart flutters within me as I look out the window at God's big world spinning beneath me—such a large circle Jesus calls us to, the largest mission field of all. I'm nearly certain this must have been how his first twelve felt too. Yet he looked them in the eyes and said, "All authority in heaven and on earth has been given to me. Go therefore and make disciples of all nations" (Matthew 28:18-19).

Go therefore. Go. Strap on your sandals; get on a horse; get your silly you on a plane and go. And as I go, my provincial governor, my me-my-we blinders, get loosened as his earth spins by slowly under my plane. Then my blinders get clean ripped off as we explode (with a shock of luggage, taxis, strange street signs and foreign words) into the ends of the earth. I find my sometimes recreational, decorative faith not fitting quite right, and I glance around looking for God, banking on that universal truth that humbled Job saw so clearly: "For he looks to the ends of the earth and sees everything under the heavens" (Job 28:24). I know taking myself to the ends of the earth would be unthinkable if God weren't already there.

The Need for Global Partnerships

It turns out Job was right: God does look to the ends of the earth. We shouldn't read our myopia or apathy onto our God: he sees everything, and cares. A quick flip through the Psalms helps us see how interested God is in every square inch of creation:

- "All the ends of the earth shall remember and turn to the LORD" (Psalm 22:27).

- " So your praise reaches to the ends of the earth" (Psalm 48:10).

- "O God of our salvation, the hope of all the ends of the earth and of the farthest seas" (Psalm 65:5).

- "Let all the ends of the earth fear him!" (Psalm 67:7).

- "May he have dominion from sea to sea . . . to the ends of the earth!" (Psalm 72:8).

- "All the ends of the earth have seen the salvation of our God" (Psalm 98:3).

This global concern motivated God to call Abraham ("and in you all the families of the earth shall be blessed," Genesis 12:3) and send out his church ("you will be my witnesses . . . to the end of the earth," Acts 1:8). This same global concern stands behind all the great mission-sending movements in the life of the church (from Calvin's Geneva to the Student Volunteer Movement to the missions-sending phenomena happening today in South Korea and Brazil). This is simply God's people getting caught up in God's work in the world—and in that sense global missions today are nothing new.

But some things are new. God has a vibrant, global church now, which has implications for global missions. For the last several generations, God's church was most prominent—or at least most conspicuous—in Europe and North America. And so global missions seemed to have a one-sided tilt to it: from the West to the rest. But now, with a growing church in Africa, Asia and South America and a declining church in Europe (and perhaps to some extent in North America as well), global missions has less of a tilt to it. God has a vibrant, global church now. So as his people get caught up in his work in the world, we see vibrant global partnerships blossoming between far-flung Christians, rather than a one-sided global missions flow.

These global partnerships are a blessing. Just as a local church is best understood as a "body" with many different unique "parts" (as Paul put it in 1 Corinthians 12), so God's global church is a single body made up of many different parts. These parts are different from each other: the church in America is quite different from the church in Africa. And these differences are good. Remember Paul's reminder that having differently made parts of a body is essential and intended: "If the whole body were an eye, where would be the sense of hearing? If the whole body were an ear, where would be the sense of smell? But as it is, God arranged the members in the body, each one of them, as he chose. If all were a single member, where would the body be? As it is, there are many parts, yet one body" (1 Corinthians 12:17-20).

What this means for God's global church is that we must work together as we get caught up together in God's work in the world. Again, Paul: "The eye cannot say to the hand, 'I have no need of you,' nor again the head to the feet, 'I have no need of you'" (1 Corinthians 12:21). The American church needs the African church; the South American church needs the Asian church. We need each other in order to function properly. And nowhere is this more palpable than when it comes to global missions.

We are on this world together, sent together by God, who is interested in every square inch. Our global partnerships will not only help us spread God's name into every square inch of creation; they will also help us maintain the healthy, affectionate, genuine unity God intends for us. As Paul wrote, "God has so composed the body . . . that there may be no division in the body, but that the members may have the same care for one another. If one member suffers, all suffer together; if one member is honored, all rejoice together" (1 Corinthians 12:24-26).

So the ends of the earth have always been an important mission field. And now—perhaps more than ever—healthy global partnerships are an important part of God's work in this world. And this has unavoidable implications for the Missional Christian.

The Role of the Missional Christian in the World

From the time Christians were first called "Christians," they have been getting caught up in God's vibrant work in the ends of the earth. In Syrian Antioch (where we were first called "Christians"), the believers had Sober Eyes that considered not only their local circles of ministry, but also the wider circles of God's concern.

When they heard that a famine was coming that would spread "over all the world," they didn't circle the wagons and make sure Antioch had enough food. Rather, seeing the need that was coming, they put their Servant Hands to use. Luke recorded their response: "So the disciples determined, every one according to his ability, to send relief to the brothers living in Judea. And they did so, sending it to the elders by the hand of Barnabas and Saul" (Acts 11:29-30).

This is the same today. As Missional Christians hear about what's going on in far lands, they are affected by it. They see the need all around as darkness and decay that God's own church, as salt and light, is called to address. And so Missional Christians give of their own money and possessions to help meet needs that happen to be far away from their own driveways.

And sometimes they actually leave their driveways, get on a plane and go put their Ready Feet on the ground right where the need is. The same was true in Antioch: "While they were worshiping the Lord and fasting, the Holy Spirit said, 'Set apart for me Barnabas and Saul for the work to which I have called them.' Then after fasting and praying they laid their hands on them and sent them off" (Acts 13:2-3). And thus began the first international mission trip. These Missional Christians had Ready Feet, so when God said go, there was no hesitation.

It's important that this going wasn't just a matter for Barnabas and Saul. The entire church was a part of this trip, their Compassionate Hearts heavily invested in what happened. We catch a glimpse of this when Barnabas and Paul returned from their trip:

Then they passed through Pisidia and came to Pamphylia. And when they had spoken the word in Perga, they went down to Attalia, and from there they sailed to Antioch, where they had been commended to the grace of God for the work that they had fulfilled. And when they arrived and gathered the church together, they declared all that God had done with them, and how he had opened a door of faith to the Gentiles. And they remained no little time with the disciples. (Acts 14:24-28)

While Barnabas and Paul did the going, those who stayed behind (doing the sending and the praying) were still heavily invested. Notice Luke's comment that they lingered for some time, hearing "*all* that God had done" on the trip. This was not a passing fad or minor program; rather, the entire church was invested and caught up in God's work in the ends of the earth. In fact, when a controversy arose about Gentiles receiving the gospel, the church in Antioch was heavily involved in the discussions, sending a contingent down to Jerusalem to ensure the gospel would continue to be preached to the ends of the earth.

This passion for God's work in the ends of the earth continues in God's church to this day. We look around with Sober Eyes at all of God's world, and we care about what we see. We are strategically generous with our money and possessions to help meet needs. We help send and support those whom God sends, and when God sends us, we go. And what do we do when we go? Exactly what our Servant Hands are used to: serving, washing dirty feet, attending to the needs of others and allowing our Compassionate Hearts to get involved in what we're doing—willing to suffer alongside others.

As we do all this praying and supporting and going, there are some very important things to keep in mind about ministry to the ends of the earth.

Five Things to Keep in Mind While Serving Overseas

1. You can be generous with your prayer and money. As Christians in the West, it is important that we recognize what is unique about our "part" of the global Christian "body": God has blessed us in extraordinary ways with money, possessions, education and social connections. While the face of global missions has changed (it's not just the West to the rest), we are still a vital part of God's global body; the body needs us, and we need the rest of the body. This means coming to terms with how resource-heavy we are and what that implies about our part in global partnerships.

For example, when we learn about the slums of the megacities around the world (when we hear about the mass of people streaming into these slums and how needy they are and how responsive they are to the gospel), we may be tempted to jump right on a plane. But we need to remember God's robust global church. My friend Will, who works with a mission agency that ministers among the urban poor around the world, explained the missional math to me this way: If you were God, who would you send to a slum filled with poor Muslims? A white-faced American believer who knows very little about survival in a slum and who would require thousands of dollars a month to send? Or a dark-faced Brazilian believer who grew up in a slum and who would require only hundreds of dollars a month to send?

Obviously God can send whomever he wants. And he does. But the humbling implications are clear: we are equipped well as Western believers in certain ways, and not in others. Will has experienced this firsthand. While living in Tegucigalpa, Honduras, he got involved with a network of poor, urban pastors who were getting caught up in God's work around the world. They wanted the church in Honduras to be a mission-sending church, but they lacked the organizational systems and sending strategies to pull it off. As a Western Christian with quite a bit of education and many connections, Will had these things in spades.

So Will helped create the missions-sending infrastructure while the Honduran pastors preached and taught and saw God raise the temperature in the Honduran church for global missions. Of course, God was in every part of this partnership. A young

Honduran woman, Julia, who had grown up in a small, rural village had heard from God in a dream years before that he was calling her to a country in northern Africa that most people reading this book would have a tough time locating on a map. She treasured this word from God in her heart, having no idea how it would happen, until she was at a church service where one of these mission-minded pastors was preaching. And today, because of a global partnership between churches in Honduras and churches in the United States, Julia is now a minister of the gospel in that country in North Africa.

In many cases, this is the shape of global missions today. That means Missional Christians in the West need to take seriously the call to be generous with financial, administrative and prayer support of God's work around the world. And we need to do this strategically, thoughtfully and humbly. It is incumbent upon us as servants not just to fling away our money to the first person who comes calling or to causes we've "always" supported, but to spend time in prayer and thought, discerning how exactly, where exactly and when exactly God is calling us to be involved in his global work. Toward this end, you might find Mary Lederleitner's *Cross-Cultural Partnerships: Navigating the Complexities of Money and Mission* very helpful.

2. Sustainability is the goal. If God calls us to spend our time, energy and prayers in a certain way, we must be obedient. It is not our place to question God's calling, but to say yes and to respond with joyful generosity and persistent prayers. Just as in Antioch, there's a reason prayer is so connected with global mission. But what do Missional Christians do when God hasn't been so specific? What do we do when we start getting caught up in God's global mission but are presented with so many seemingly worthwhile ministries to partner with? There are weeks that it seems everyone could use more money and connections and prayers— but not every week does God specifically direct us in where to do our giving and praying. This is where we need to be good stewards of what God has generously entrusted to us by giving it away in ways that are strategic and wise. This means careful thought.

When I arrived at Bonhomme as the minister of outreach, I was pleased to hear about a blossoming partnership between Bonhomme members and a small Christian orphanage in Honduras. It was clear that God was moving several members to get caught up in God's work in this humble orphanage on the outskirts of Tegucigalpa, and that God was calling the amazing folks who ran the orphanage to be involved with our church family. There was just one problem: some of those at Bonhomme wanted to see our church start funding the orphanage's monthly budget—in its entirety. This goal was motivated by love and affection, but wasn't guided by strategy.

I checked with a missionary friend in Tegucigalpa, and she assured me that taking over the monthly bills would be the worst thing we could do for the orphanage. She said our goal should be to give in ways that helped develop sustainability, not dependency. We should add more "legs" to their "stool," not create a stool with one big leg. That, she said, was a recipe for dependency and disaster.

So she encouraged us to pursue our other goals, which were equally well-intentioned but also happened to be way more strategic. So we designed a sponsorship program in which over twenty Bonhomme families would each sponsor one of the children in the orphanage. This brought many more legs under the stool of the orphanage. We eventually helped them build a new bakery so they could expand their microenterprise and create more self-generated income. And we are now working on ways of getting more churches in their own city to partner in their ministry.

It's this kind of sustainable ministry that ought to be our goal when trying to determine giving priorities. Unfortunately this means more work: research, thought and dialogue take time. But it's time well spent. On a recent trip to Ethiopia, I got to see the strategic work of a locally run ministry firsthand by visiting remote Muslim villages. These villages are being transformed by the humble work of vibrant, young teacher-missionaries whose annual salaries are much less than the monthly salaries of many missionaries I know. That knowledge made me recommit myself to the hard work of doing my own giving (and helping my church do its corporate giving) in ways that are strategic. For more on making your giving wise and strategic, read *When Helping Hurts: Alleviating Poverty Without Hurting the Poor . . . and Ourselves* by Steve Corbett and Brian Fikkert or Robert Lupton's *Toxic Charity: How Churches and Charities Hurt Those They Help (And How to Reverse It)*.

3. *It's all about partnership*. Even though the face of missions has shifted significantly, we in the West can have a hard time kicking our outdated mission habits. When we perceived global missions as being from the West to the rest, we developed a certain posture, perhaps unknowingly: the posture of the beneficent donor. But this paternalistic posture (I'm here to help you, you are here to be helped by me) does not come in handy when developing a global partnership. Partners are equals. Partners are doing something together. Partners need each other. We can unfortunately become so focused on the resources we're bringing to the table that we are blind to what our global partners are bringing to the table.

Several years ago, I was in Buenos Aires doing a "pre-trip" for one of InterVarsity's fairly intense Global Urban Treks. Two of us from InterVarsity had gone down to Argentina to look for a few viable ministry partnerships in some of the many slum communities in Buenos Aires. Not only were we "interviewing" potential partners, but they were "interviewing" us as well. On one of these visits I was reminded, in an unforgettable way, just what partnership is all about.

We were in the middle of one of the slums (or "villas" as they call them in Buenos Aires) and had found the ministry site we were looking for: it was a cobbled-together set of buildings on a prominent corner of the poor community. Inside we heard the sound of children. They were there for a tutoring program, and they were eating what might be, we were told, the only meal they would get that day. The children seemed calm and joyful, and the smell of fresh bread was a welcome break from the smell of garbage out in the street. As we watched the children return to their lessons, the director of the ministry walked in the door.

He was a bear of a man—over six feet tall, heavy and with a wide and genuine smile. But what was immediately striking was a large growth on the side of his neck, a growth that had to be a quarter of the size of his head. Here was a humble man, in tattered clothes and wearing no shoes, who had to carry this deformity through life. My instinct was to feel sorry for him. But as he took us on a walking tour of the villa, I grew more and more impressed with him. Everyone we passed greeted him with obvious affection, and the comments he made about the slum community were insightful and strategic. Though he had never finished school, he had grown up in this very slum—and knew this place inside and out.

By the end of the tour, when we stood outside the ministry building chatting, two things had become crystal clear to me: First, I understood in detail how our finances and summer interns could make a real difference for this ministry going forward. Second, and more importantly, I knew we could do nothing in this villa without the expertise, connections and instincts of this barefooted man standing before me. It was tempting for me, on a surface level, to look at the two of us and think I was the one (educated, financed, resourced) who was doing the helping. But that couldn't have been further from the truth. We were true equals standing there in that garbage-strewn street.

And that, it turns out, is what partnership is all about. One of the most helpful books I have ever read on nurturing healthy global partnership is the small, practical *Building Strategic Rela-*

tionships: A Practical Guide to Partnering with Non-Western Missions by Daniel Rickett. The book is worth the cover price just for the practical checklists it provides.

4. You can cross cultures with grace and humility. No matter how servant-hearted and internationally savvy you may be, crossing cultures is tricky. Experiencing stress and culture shock is unavoidable. If you are in another culture for any significant amount of time, you will struggle with the new culture. But it is possible to cross cultures with grace and humility.

As Duane Elmer points out in *Cross-Cultural Connections: Stepping Out and Fitting In Around the World*, our posture as we enter a new culture is crucial. Experience and research bear out

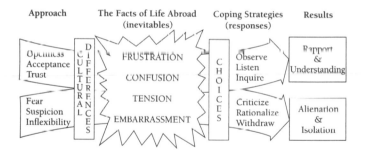

The Cultural Adjustment Map (From Duane Elmer, *Cross-Cultural Connections* [Downers Grove, Ill.: InterVarsity Press, 2002], p. 72.)

that if you step into a new culture with a posture of suspicion, fear, superiority or prejudice, you will respond to inevitable tensions with the new culture by isolating yourself, criticizing and rationalizing. This will always land you somewhere very ugly and unhappy. But if you step into a new culture with a servant's posture (open, accepting, trusting, adaptable), you will find yourself responding to inevitable differences in culture by observing, inquiring, listening and initiating. This leads somewhere much more beautiful.

It is one thing to have Servant Hands in your first day in another culture; it's quite another to maintain a servant posture when you're tired of hearing unfamiliar words, tired of everything looking different and smelling different and tasting different, tired of not fully understanding and not fully being understood. In those moments of cultural dissonance, it can be tempting to criticize (Why do they do everything "wrong" here?), fantasize (What I wouldn't give for a Big Mac right now!), grab for every ounce of control and comfort you can get (I don't care if everyone has to wait—I am taking a hot shower!) and survive (Exactly how many hours until I'm on the plane home?).

A few years back, Maureen was giving me a tour of Infiernito, a small, isolated neighborhood outside Tegucigalpa. Infiernito is so notorious as a dangerous, poor neighborhood that our Honduran guides were uncomfortable taking us into the area (the nickname Infiernito means "little hell"). During this tour I saw two sides of the spectrum of how Christians can cross cultures.

On one side was Maureen. She walked some friends and me through the streets of Infiernito, beginning at a complex of small microenterprises she had helped develop and ending at her humble home in the heart of Infiernito. Along the way we stopped off at the local school, where she was embraced by local children and where the principal discussed some decisions with Maureen. Later our dirt path brought us near a co-op daycare developed so that the single mothers of the neighborhood could work. All in all, we were floored by how Maureen had incarnated into the neighborhood. She had adapted to the local culture and obviously really loved this community. In return she was surrounded by rich relationships. Seeing Maureen in Infiernito was beautiful.

On the other side of the spectrum was a group of American Christians Maureen was hosting. As Maureen and I sat in her small pickup truck, waiting for this group to join us for the day's events, she expressed her disappointment in how the group was handling the differences in culture. They had not entered In-fiernito with grace and humility, but with a certain amount of fear and prejudice. She was noticing that even after only a few days, they were isolating themselves, not eagerly initiating conversations with locals. And they had begun spending more time on their own comfort: taking a long time to get ready and lingering over their meals. Seeing this group in Infiernito was not beautiful; it was a bit painful.

Now, in one sense, the differences make complete sense: Maureen was a long-term missionary living full time in this new culture, whereas the others were short-termers, many of them crossing cultures for the first time. There's nothing surprising about this. But it has become for me an image of the options open to us when we cross cultures: We can cross cultures with grace and humility, with a servant's posture. Or we can cross cultures with fear and suspicion. Our entry posture makes all the difference in the world. Because of this we all ought to grow in our ability to cross cultures well; this isn't something we innately know how to do, but it's something we can learn and grow in.

Toward that end, I highly recommend working through *Ministering Crossculturally: An Incarnational Model for Personal Relationships* by Marvin K. Mayers and Sherwood G. Lingenfelter. When I am preparing teams to go overseas, I often have them read *Mack & Leeann's Guide to Short-Term Missions* by Mack and Leeann Stiles.

5. Even limited language acquisition can open important doors. Sometimes when we are partnering with God's church in the ends of the earth, we are not only gifted differently (as different parts of the body), we also speak different languages. In chapter two ("Servant Hands"), we saw how the servant posture relates to language: as servants patterned after Jesus, we are called to incarnate ourselves, and so we make attempts to learn another language rather than assuming everyone should learn ours. Because English is such a widespread language and because learning even a few foreign phrases takes work, this is an element of crosscultural servanthood that we often ignore. We do this to our detriment. When crossing cultures, even limited language acquisition can make a huge difference.

Years ago, I had been living in Mexico for only a week or so and was brand new to Spanish. It was my first international missions trip, and so a friend and I had decided to go into the summer working together on learning some basic phrases in Spanish. Two weeks in, I had a smattering of words and bits of Spanish phrases rolling around in my head as we sat down for a late dinner with our host family. We had just met this vibrant Christian family and gone to an evening church service together. And now we were back, sitting down to dinner together. The father turned to me and asked me in rough English if I would pray for our meal.

I hesitated. Everyone else on my team spoke better Spanish than I did—shouldn't one of them pray the prayer? Or perhaps I could just pray in English? That'd be easier, and God speaks English too. But a look and smile from my team leader helped me understand: we were here as servants. I should give it a try. So I awkwardly began saying a simple prayer. *"Gracias, Dios."* That means "Thanks, God"—I picked that one up at the church service. Let's see . . . everyone's waiting. What can I thank God for? *"Por . . . "* Good. That means "for." Maybe I can thank God for the church service. "Church" is *iglesia*, but "service"? Can I just add an *O* or *A* at the end? I finished my prayer: *"por la cervesa a la iglesia."* And with a confident "Amen," I concluded the prayer. I had done it!

Hadn't I?

My team leader was smiling a bit as he began eating. I leaned to my friend next to me. "Hey, what exactly did I pray?" And then I was told that I had just thanked God for the beer at the church.

Turns out "service" is *servicio*, but everyone in that part of the country referred to "church services" as *cultos*. My face turned as red as the setting sun as we all burst out laughing at this simple mistake.

This laughter broke the ice with our new host family and paved the way for natural conversation and quickly forming fellowship.

Even learning a few phrases makes a huge difference in breaking the ice and helping form friendships, but that's not all basic language acquisition does. Making the effort to learn even twenty or so basic words and phrases opens several doors. It certainly breaks the ice and helps in the early stages of making friends crossculturally, but it also shows respect for the receiving culture. Even when our attempts are silly and incorrect (as is often the case), our hosts aren't offended that we got the word wrong; they are usually moved that we are making an effort. It shows that we take their culture seriously and are making an effort, like Christ, to come in as servants.

It also puts us in the posture of a learner. This not only helps us genuinely enter into a culture with humility (it's hard not to be humble when you thank God for the beer or call yourself a taco), but also provides a tangible place for those we are partnering with to lead us and teach us. This is an effective antidote for the vestigial paternalism we often default to. Making an effort in this practical area also provides a window into the culture you are going into; language and culture are inextricably intertwined, and learning even a small bit of language forces you to begin thinking like those in the other culture.

So, as servants, we make an attempt at language—even if it's just the basics and even if we have translators alongside us doing most of the heavy lifting. On a couple of recent trips to Russia, I was thrilled to have translators with us the entire time; they became good friends and made our global partnership possible. But nothing can replace looking a kid in the eye and being able to ask, in his language, what his name is. (*Kak vaz za-vut?*) And so, even with translators, we memorize and struggle with pronunciation and take a stab. We learn—even late at night when the language part of our brain has become exhausted. This is what servants do.

On a recent trip to Ethiopia, I put in a little bit of time learning twenty basic words and phrases in Amharic, the official national language. Amharic is probably the hardest language I've ever tried my hand at. But a few days into our trip, we were on a van ride out to a remote village where we would get on horseback and make our way up to some really remote villages. I was told then that most people in those villages would speak only Oromo. Sigh. As I sat in the van, I wanted to give up. We had translators along, so why should I make an effort at the tribal language?

A smile and nod from our trip leader, Caroline, got my attention, and she suggested I learn some Oromo from Gemechu, one of the Ethiopians going up with us. And so I did, jotting down little phrases as Gemechu taught them to me. And here's the thing: not only did this create a bond between Gemechu and me (up to then we had been awkwardly sitting quietly next to each other in the van), but as it turned out, our group got fairly spread out on our miles-long horse ride and toward the end I got grouped in with some local riders—my horse deciding that it wanted to gallop along for the sprint to the end.

When the sprint ended, I was a bit rattled. And when I stepped down from my horse and looked around, I realized I was the only one from my group who had arrived in the small village. So there I was, surrounded by a group of forty men: serious-looking shepherds and elders from the village who were there to greet us. Guess what language they all spoke? That's right. I pulled out my notes and made some basic greetings in Oromo, which immediately broke the ice and gave us a place to start. Though we were from two very different cultures (they all had shepherds crooks with them; I had a fanny pouch with hand sanitizer), my imperfect attempts at their language brought us closer together. Don't get me wrong. I was certainly glad when our interpreters arrived ten minutes later, but I was amazed at how a little work on phrases in the van made such a difference.

Some people will want to lean into language and take courses and work with sophisticated and effective language software. But if you are looking for a very basic start, I've found the Lonely Planet phrasebooks to be fabulous resources. They fit in your pocket, are arranged in intuitive sections and have two-way dictionaries in the back. Spend a couple of hours with one of those or a language app on your phone, and you'll be well on your way.

Serving the Ends of the Earth

Just as Jesus asked his small-town, provincial disciples to go to the ends of the earth, so God asks every believer (at some point) to get caught up in his work somewhere far away. This is part of what it means to be in God's robust, global church. Just like those Christians in Antioch, we pray, we care, we give, we send and (when God nudges us) we go to be a part of God's work in faraway places.

Interestingly, many scholars believe Luke was from the city of Antioch and became a Christian there. So, the one who wrote the Gospel of Luke and the book of Acts (which chronicles the inexorable spread of Christianity from Jerusalem through Judea into Samaria and out to the ends of the earth) was not only *marked by* God's concern for every square inch (when the gospel was brought to Antioch), but got *caught up in* that concern as well (going with Paul on some journeys and eventually writing Luke and Acts).

As Christians in the West, it is tempting to live in a cultural ghetto. Though the world is in many ways coming to us, it can still be tempting to avoid other cultures (ignore them and, often, criticize them) rather than learn the beautiful gospel ballet of engaging in crosscultural ministry. Even when we go out of the country, it is tempting to spend our time enclosed in self-contained bubbles of American culture (Cancun anyone?) or to venture out to *look at* other cultures without really *engaging* them. But Missional Christians, caught up as they are in God's work in every corner of this world as members of God's robust, global church, find themselves caring about faraway places and people just as God does.

And the more we partner with God in this way, the more our myopic blinders are taken off and the more our xenophobic apathy begins to wear off. We find ourselves praying and giving and sending and caring and traveling in this beautiful, messy, miraculous work of crosscultural ministry. In the process we are changed. In fact, there are ways that being a part of a global partnership affects and changes you that no other Christian service can. This is a gift.

As your own blinders are taken off, you will likely find Meic Pearse's *Why the Rest Hates the West: Understanding the Roots of Global Rage* to be quite helpful. Also, a great overview of this area of the missional life can be found in *Cross-Cultural Servanthood: Serving the World in Christlike Humility* by Duane Elmer.

There's something about looking out an airplane window and seeing God's world spin slowly beneath you. We will never get crossing cultures perfect, of course. There's just always something wonderfully dizzying about waking up in your own comfortable bed one morning and lying down later that night (or the next? Time zones can be confusing) in a faraway place where everything seems just a little bit "off."

But more glorious and memorable than the most quirky and humorous crosscultural blunders you will make is that ineffable feeling of standing with a brother or sister in Christ who comes from a very different place in the world, as you labor together, caught up all together in God's work in this wide, wide world of his.

Conclusion

The Missional Motivation

• • •

IF YOU'VE MADE YOUR WAY to this page the hard way (reading every page that's led up to it), I imagine you might be feeling a bit overwhelmed right now—especially after working through the second half of the book, "Geography." There are a whole lot of "square inches" in this world where we could be joyfully caught up in God's work. There's no lack of places for us to *go and do likewise*. And considering them all at once can lead to a bit of spiritual vertigo.

The good news for Missional Christians is that we have a good shepherd who is leading us forward. He knows us by name, and loves us. He wants us to grow and feel the joy of his labor. Jesus knew intimately the sustenance that comes from doing the Father's will; it was like food, he said. And the same is true for us.

So enjoy the missional life! Take the next step God has for you to take. Don't become so overwhelmed by all the possibilities that you stay frozen and immobile. Ask God to point to one place for you to begin, and start there. It's his work after all, so allow him to take you along step by step. Don't try doing everything at once.

But don't settle for too little either. Unfortunately it takes very little to be seen as a saint these days. Even a small amount of service (a mere dip into the city, just a whisper of Jesus' name in conversation, a small donation to a cause—tax deductible, of course) garners a large amount of applause from the people around us. This creates a context for Christians I call the Two-Inch Olympics.

To get an idea of the Two-Inch Olympics, imagine a large stadium, its seats filled with cheering, applauding, sign-waving fans. And the athletes down on the track? Well, they are racing and jumping over hurdles and waving to the crowd in victory. But there's just one thing wrong with the picture: the hurdles are only two inches high. Same with the high jump. Here are these fit athletes capable of jumping high and long just barely clearing two inches. But with each "successful," underwhelming jump, the crowd goes wild. And the athletes become convinced they are doing amazing things on the field.

This is the Two-Inch Olympics. And this is the context some Missional Christians find themselves in. As a result, we might be tempted to get caught up in God's work in the world just a little bit. We serve, but just enough service to look good on a résumé. We go on a service trip or two—and the world is awed by our meager, metered-out acts of service. The crowd goes wild as we clear two-inch hurdles and high jumps. And so it is mighty tempting to settle as a Missional Christian even though you're just getting started.

But here's a beautiful thing: there's someone in the stadium who's not cheering. Jesus stands among us looking confused by the ways we uproariously applaud for such meager faithfulness. He knows, after all, what we are capable of. He knows that we are designed to jump high and long, to run fast and hard. And his Spirit comes among us to inspire, to equip, to impassion, to blow so hard on our sleepy spirits that we find ourselves joyfully caught up in the race of our lives, able to do so much more than we had ever imagined. This is what it means to be a Missional Christian.

We are not meant to live safe, happy, successful Christian lives. Though it is painful and involves suffering, it is in laying our lives down that we actually find life. Why endeavor to be a Missional Christian? For the joy of it! This is where true life is found, as Jesus himself modeled for us. When we settle for safety or happiness or success we are doing just that—settling. Why lean against the temptation to jump over two-inch hurdles? Because we are designed to run hard and fast, to jump long and high, to share joyfully in our Father's work. We are not meant to live lives that will be soon forgotten, but lives that are used by God to change this world.

The author of Hebrews calls out to us across the centuries: "Let us run with endurance the race that is set before us, looking to Jesus, the founder and perfecter of our faith, who for the joy that was set before him endured the cross, despising the shame, and is seated at the right hand of the throne of God" (Hebrews 12:1-2).

We are to look to Jesus as our model. For it is in Jesus himself that we find our ultimate motivation for mission, as the great Scottish preacher James S. Stewart reminds us:

> In the last resort, the one reason for missions is *Christ*. He only is the motive, God's presence in him the one sufficient cause. The fact is, belief in missions and belief in Christ stand and fall together. To say, "I believe that God so loved the world that in Christ he gave everything He had, gave His very self," to use such words not lightly or conventionally but in spirit and in truth, means that the one who uses them binds himself irrevocably to make self-giving the controlling principle of life: and this is the very essence of mission.
>
> To put it otherwise, the concern for world evangelization is not something tacked on to a man's personal Christianity, which he may take or leave as he chooses: it is rooted inde-

feasibly in the character of the God who has come to us in Jesus. Thus it can never be the province of a few enthusiasts, a sideline or specialty of those who happen to have a bent that way. It is the distinctive mark of being a Christian. To accept Christ is to enlist under a missionary banner.

As for me, I am so glad I accepted Christ. And I am so glad God helped me see that this meant I had enlisted under a missionary banner. I'm glad God began showing me how to *go and do*. And I'm glad that as I do all this *going*, I can fix my eyes on Jesus, who has left a model for us all.

May we all run with endurance the race God has marked out for us. And as we pick up speed, let us grow and learn and not be afraid of making mistakes. God never asks us to be perfect, just faithful. Don't wait around reading books about missions until you are "ready." That day will never come. Instead, dive right in. And then your desire to learn and grow will shoot through the roof. Then your reading will take on a new urgency. Jesus believed in on-the-job-training for his disciples. And still does.

May we get caught up—every one of us, more and more every year—in the work of our God. No matter what it does to our anatomy. No matter where it takes us geographically. The word *missional* might be grammatically awkward. And the term *Missional Christian* might be a bit redundant. But I pray this term, along with this whole book, helps us all see, anew, everything God has in store for us.

I can barely believe what has happened inside me and around me these last few decades since God first asked me to *go and do*. And I can barely wait to see what happens in the next.

Now it's your turn. Go and do likewise.

Acknowledgments

● ● ●

IF AT ANY POINT IN THIS BOOK you found yourself
tiring of my incessant recommendation of other books to read for
more "in-depth analysis," you perhaps have the beginning of a
sense of how indebted I am to the many scholars and practitioners
whose work has informed me and shaped my missional thinking
and practice over the years. The "Recommended Books" section
that follows is an apt acknowledgment of these brothers and sisters.

You may also have noticed that I spent a fair amount of time
telling the story of my own journey from being a self-isolating Safe
Christian to a fumbling but joyful Missional Christian. If there
were any parts of that story that made you flinch and wonder at
my bumbling ways, this is likely due to my own weaknesses. If
there were any parts of my story that made you smile, this is likely
due to God's gentle work inside me (in spite of my hesitations) and
the patient, wise influence of four communities of faith.

These four communities have been handmaidens of God's work
in my life, used powerfully to heal, grow, guide, educate, train and
generally shape me. I am who I am because of these four communities of faith. And so I thank them:

Young Life, for showing me a skit about an orange and helping
me grab hold of Jesus. Special thanks to Ben, Todd, Bobby and Patty.

InterVarsity Christian Fellowship, for inviting me to grow up and being so consistently patient with such a reticent disciple, servant and leader. Special thanks to Troy, Sue and Larry; Al, Scott and Bob; and Megan, Dulcy and Ryan.

Hillside Church of the Savior, for teaching me about the power and sufficiency of the unadorned Word of God. Special thanks to Gene, Kevin and Stan.

Bonhomme Presbyterian Church, for asking me to take everything I've learned and run with it. Special thanks to Tom, that risk-taking search committee and all my fellow Hobbits in the House of Elrond.

Discussion Questions

• • •

Introduction: *Missional* **Is Not a Word**

1. Read Luke 10:25-37. Would you agree that Jesus' words to the lawyer (go and do likewise) are "bothersome"?

2. The introduction suggests there are four basic postures Christians take toward the world around them. Which of these postures is most common in the Christians around you?

3. Are you more tempted to be a Safe Christian, Successful Christian or Happy Christian?

4. What pictures come to mind when you hear the word *missionary*? Do you see yourself as a missionary?

5. A Missional Christian is defined as a Christian who is marked by God's work in this world and caught up in that work as well. Do you find this definition to be helpful?

Chapter 1: Sober Eyes

1. Read Matthew 5:13-17. Do you agree that Jesus' call to be salt and light implies that this world we're in is decaying and dark?

2. Generally speaking, how would you characterize your own eyes (Fearful, Eager, Recreational, Sober)? What kind of eyes are you tempted to have on a bad week?

3. Think back over your past week. What needs did you see around you? How did these make you feel? Overall, would you describe yourself as more attentive or more dull to the needs around you?

4. Do you see yourself as blessed to be a blessing? How have you been a blessing over the last year?

5. How do you normally think of the Psalms? Flip through a few psalms and then ask, how might praying these psalms be particularly helpful for those with Sober Eyes?

Chapter 2: Servant Hands

1. Read John 13:3-17. When Jesus told his disciples to wash each other's feet, what do you think he meant by that? How broadly should we understand this "washing of feet" today?

2. Generally speaking, how would you characterize your own hands (Defensive, Grabby, Giddy, Servant)? What kind of hands are you tempted to have on a bad week?

3. How can we understand generosity with possessions as a form of serving?

4. What do you find compelling or problematic about the brief description of servant-hearted evangelism, where we apply Jesus' words "As you wish that others would do to you . . ." to our non-Christian friends?

5. How common is fasting among your friends? In your own life? How do you think fasting might be a particularly helpful discipline for people with Servant Hands?

Chapter 3: Ready Feet

1. Read Acts 1:6-9. This chapter suggests that the disciples' geographic marching orders (Jerusalem, Judea, Samaria, the ends of the earth) are not only historical but also somewhat normative for every Christian. What problems or possibilities do you see in this position?

2. Generally speaking, how would you characterize your own feet (Cautious, Ambitious, Skipping, Ready)? On a bad week, what kind of feet are you tempted to have?

3. Do you agree that God is interested in "every square inch" of creation? Why, or why not? Using the four geographic circles, map out your own Jerusalem, Judea, Samaria and ends of the earth.

4. Has God ever nudged you to go somewhere that was difficult or uncomfortable for you to go? How did it turn out?

5. Do you have many experiences relating crossculturally? How would you describe these interactions (uncomfortable, exciting, painful, awkward, fascinating, eye-opening, humbling . . .)?

Chapter 4: Compassionate Heart

1. Read Matthew 6:19-21. Do you have any recent experiences with physical belongings being stolen, broken or misplaced? If so, how did that experience leave you feeling?

2. Compare the different "investment strategies" characterized in the opening of the chapter. Using this language, where would you say most of your treasure is stored? Have you found that your heart has followed your treasure?

3. Jesus said, "Blessed are those who mourn." What do you find helpful, challenging or problematic with this chapter's treatment of this beatitude?

4. Describe your relationship to the discipline of worship. Do you feel a need for worship in your life? Do you think becoming more missional could really affect your experience of worship?

5. Read Matthew 21:28-31. Do you think you should "have a heart" for a people or a cause before getting involved?

Chapter 5: Joyful Soul

1. Read Mark 8:34-35. How are we to understand and think of

"taking up your cross" in a context where literal crucifixion is not really in play? Is suffering optional, guaranteed, something a Christian can control?

2. We're given some very different pictures in this chapter of how Safe, Successful, Happy and Missional Christians relate with God. Which description(s) comes closest to matching up with your relationship with God?

3. Do you think it is always the case that becoming more missional produces spiritual growth (pruning) and increased attack?

4. What's your most recent experience of being "pruned" by God? In what ways was it painful? Was it worth it? Did it result in more "fruit" in your life?

5. Have you ever taken a retreat of silence? If so, how did it affect your relationship with God? Did you find yourself more able to serve afterward? If not, how do you think such a discipline would feel for you? Does it sound attractive or difficult?

Chapter 6: Purposeful Family

1. In this chapter, the "whole family" is defined as "a conglomerate of the family I was born into, the family I am creating with my wife, and my inner circle of friends." What five words would you use to describe your own "whole family"?

2. Are there any ways you behave differently when you are with your family? How would you describe your own "blind spots"?

3. Forgiveness, truth speaking and mercy are highlighted as common ways of serving our family members. Do you see a need for any of these in your own family?

4. What do you think of the claim that in the West we're tempted to hand our children off to others? How do you think the church and parents are meant to partner and work together in the spiritual development of children?

5. If you are a parent, how would you characterize or describe your spiritual leadership of your children?

Chapter 7: Relational Evangelism

1. There are a few different reasons given for why some Christians hesitate to see themselves as witnesses. Do you resonate with any of these hesitations?

2. How would you evaluate the claim that relational evangelism is arguably the best way for people to hear about Jesus?

3. What are the key cultural "postmodern" shifts that are highlighted? Do you see evidence of these shifts in the people around you?

4. Who are the two non-Christians you are closest to? What do you think it means to serve each of them practically?

5. If conversion is "a mysterious, organic journey," how should that affect how we approach evangelism? Is this how you currently approach evangelism?

Chapter 8: Thriving Church

1. What are five words you would use to describe "the Christian church"? What are five words you would use to describe your own local church?

2. Read 1 Corinthians 12:1-27. How does this body language fit with your own understanding of and experience of the church? To what extent has the two-part view of church (there are professionals and there are the rest of us) colored your view of church?

3. Make a list of the unmet needs in your own church. Ask God who he might be calling to meet those needs.

4. How important do you think spiritual gifts are to the health of the church? Do you have a sense of what your own spiritual gifts are?

5. What do you think of the Paul-Timothy model of mentoring? Have you ever been in such a relationship? Is there a potential "Timothy" in your life whom you could start to encourage in the faith?

Chapter 9: Urban Mercy

1. If you live in a city, what five words would you use to describe your city? If you don't live in a city, how would you describe the city closest to you? Do you have a generally positive or negative view of that city?

2. Describe what you think makes for a healthy ministry partnership between those going into the city to serve and those already in the city? If you are already involved in a partnership, how healthy would you say it is? How healthy does your partner think it is?

3. It's suggested in this chapter that those serving in the city need to go in as learners. What are some of the lessons they might learn?

4. Which stereotypes are most prevalent in the city nearest you? Make a list of the crosscultural relationships you are in personally. How would you describe those relationships?

5. Do you think systemic change and renewal are needed in your city? Make a list of examples. Do you think change and renewal are possible?

Chapter 10: Global Partnerships

1. What's your own view of God's global church? How informed are you about the Christian church in other countries?

2. Do you agree that the resource-heavy church in the West has a special role when it comes to generosity? What might it mean to take that role seriously? What are the key pitfalls to avoid?

3. What are the potential benefits and challenges of international Christian partnerships?

4. Study the "Cultural Adjustment Map." What international experiences have you had? Did you notice a connection between your entry posture and the quality of your time in the other culture?

5. Have you ever learned a second language? If so, how would you describe that learning process? What are the various benefits that can come from even limited language acquisition?

Conclusion

1. Given our "Two-Inch Olympics" context (it takes very little service to be seen as saints), evaluate your own penchant for settling, for doing a small amount of service and stopping. How can you make sure you don't settle?

2. What is the race God has in front of you right now? How healthy and servant-hearted is your service?

3. Is God calling you to take steps into a new geographic area? What hesitations do you have? What are a few first practical steps you could take?

4. Pray that God would help you run the race set before you.

5. Pick one or two books that you could read to help inform your missional development (see "Recommended Reading").

Recommended Reading

• • •

THE NATURE OF READING a short book on a wide topic is that it leaves you feeling hungry for more. Slightly dissatisfied even. If *Go and Do* has been an appetizer, merely whetting your appetite and putting you in the mood for a full meal, I feel I have done my job well. This is why I have pointed the way, throughout this book, to more than forty other books that can give you additional, more meaty and in-depth analyses of the various topics addressed.

There are, thankfully, a great number of books on the topic of getting involved in God's mission in the world, including books that address topics I haven't even touched on, such as mission as vocation, mission and the marketplace, and creation care. Here I recommend books specific to our topic at hand: becoming a Missional Christian.

Missional Theology

If you are looking for an overall theology of Christian missions, I highly recommend anything by Christopher J. H. Wright—in particular his two books *The Mission of God: Unlocking the Bible's Grand Narrative* (Downers Grove, Ill.: InterVarsity Press, 2006) and *The Mission of God's People: A Biblical Theology of the Church's Mission* (Grand Rapids: Zondervan, 2010). These two books are not only profound in their theology, but also quite readable—and important to read. Please do.

Missional Spirituality

In exploring the anatomy of a Missional Christian in part one, there were a few books that I recommended for exploring various spiritual disciplines that turn out to be essential for the ongoing health of the Missional Christian.

Practicing Praying the Psalms
James W. Sire, *Learning to Pray Through the Psalms* (Downers Grove, Ill.: InterVarsity Press, 2005).

Practicing Fasting
Lynne M. Baab, *Fasting: Spiritual Freedom Beyond Our Appetites* (Downers Grove, Ill.: InterVarsity Press, 2006).

Practicing Submission
Richard J. Foster, *Celebration of Discipline: The Path to Spiritual Growth* (San Francisco: HarperSanFrancisco, 1988).

Practicing Silence and Solitude
Ruth Haley Barton, *Invitation to Solitude and Silence: Experiencing God's Transforming Presence*, exp. ed. (Downers Grove, Ill.: InterVarsity Press, 2010).

Missional Practice

In the second half of the book, we drilled down into the practicalities of a few specific mission contexts. In each chapter I identified the basic contours of some missional practices to keep in mind and recommended further reading for those who wish to explore these contexts in greater detail. (They are listed here in the order in which they appeared in this book.)

Purposeful Family
Henri J. M. Nouwen, *The Wounded Healer: Ministry in Contem-*

porary Society (New York: Image, 1979).

M. Scott Peck, *The Road Less Traveled: A New Psychology of Love, Traditional Values and Spiritual Growth*, 25th anniv. ed. (New York: Touchstone, 2003).

Larry Crabb and Dan B. Allender, *Encouragement: The Key to Caring* (Grand Rapids: Zondervan, 1990).

Robbie F. Castleman, *Parenting in the Pew: Guiding Your Children into the Joy of Worship* (Downers Grove, Ill.: InterVarsity Press, 2002)

Dr. Scott Turansky and Joanne Miller, *Parenting Is Heart Work* (Colorado Springs: David C. Cook, 2005).

Michelle Anthony, *Spiritual Parenting: An Awakening for Today's Families* (Colorado Springs: David C. Cook, 2010).

Reggie Joiner, *Think Orange: Imagine the Impact When Church and Family Collide . . .* (Colorado Springs: David C. Cook, 2009).

Timothy Smith, *The Danger of Raising Nice Kids: Preparing Our Children to Change Their World* (Downers Grove, Ill.: InterVarsity Press, 2006).

George Barna, *Revolutionary Parenting: Raising Your Kids to Become Spiritual Champions* (Carol Stream, Ill.: Tyndale , 2010).

Relational Evangelism

James Choung, *True Story: A Christianity Worth Believing In* (Downers Grove, Ill.: InterVarsity Press, 2008).

Don Everts, *Jesus with Dirty Feet: A Down-to-Earth Look at Christianity for the Curious and Skeptical* (Downers Grove, Ill.: InterVarsity Press, 1999).

L. Singlehurst, *Sowing, Reaping, Keeping: People-Sensitive Evangelism* (Nottingham, U.K.: Inter-Varsity Press, 2006).

Lesslie Newbigin, *Proper Confidence: Faith, Doubt, and Certainty in Christian Discipleship* (Grand Rapids: Eerdmans, 1995).

Gordon T. Smith, *Beginning Well: Christian Conversion and Authentic Transformation* (Downers Grove, Ill.: InterVarsity Press, 2001).

Don Everts and Doug Schaupp, *I Once Was Lost: What Postmodern Skeptics Taught Us About Their Path to Jesus* (Downers Grove, Ill.: InterVarsity Press, 2008).

Thriving Church

Charles R. Swindoll, *Improving Your Serve: The Art of Unselfish Living*, rev. ed. (Nashville: Thomas Nelson, 1997).

Marva J. Dawn, *Powers, Weakness, and the Tabernacling of God* (Grand Rapids: Eerdmans, 2001).

R. Paul Stevens, *Spiritual Gifts*, LifeGuide Bible Studies (Downers Grove, Ill.: InterVarsity Press, 2004).

Henri J. M. Nouwen, *In the Name of Jesus: Reflections on Christian Leadership* (New York: Crossroad, 1992).

Dietrich Bonhoeffer, *Life Together: A Discussion of Christian Fellowship* (New York: HarperOne, 1978).

Jean Vanier, *Community and Growth* (Mahwah, N.J.: Paulist Press, 1989).

Richard C. Lamb Jr., *The Pursuit of God in the Company of Friends* (Downers Grove, Ill.: InterVarsity Press, 2003).

Robert Coleman, *The Master Plan of Evangelism*, abridged (Grand Rapids: Revell, 1994).

Urban Mercy

Robert D. Lupton, *Theirs Is the Kingdom: Celebrating the Gospel in Urban America* (New York: HarperOne, 1989).

Ronald J. Sider, John M. Perkins, Wayne L. Gordon and F. Albert Tizon, *Linking Arms, Linking Lives: How Urban-Suburban Partnerships Can Transform Communities* (Grand Rapids: Baker, 2008).

Mike Sares, *Pure Scum: The Left-Out, the Right-Brained and the Grace of God* (Downers Grove, Ill.: InterVarsity Press, 2010).

Spencer Perkins and Chris Rice, *More Than Equals: Racial Healing for the Sake of the Gospel*, rev. ed. (Downers Grove, Ill.: InterVarsity Press, 2000).

Paula Harris and Doug Schaupp, *Being White: Finding Our Place in a Multiethnic World* (Downers Grove, Ill.: InterVarsity Press, 2004).

Kevin Blue, *Practical Justice: Living Off-Center in a Self-Centered World* (Downers Grove, Ill.: InterVarsity Press, 2006).

Randy White, *Encounter God in the City: Onramps to Personal and Community Transformation* (Downers Grove, Ill.: InterVarsity Press, 2006).

Harvie M. Conn and Manuel Ortiz, *Urban Ministry: The Kingdom, the City and the People of God* (Downers Grove, Ill.: InterVarsity Press, 2002).

Randy White, *Journey to the Center of the City: Making a Difference in an Urban Neighborhood* (Downers Grove, Ill.: InterVarsity Press, 1996).

Robert D. Lupton, *Renewing the City: Reflections on Community Development and Urban Renewal* (Downers Grove, Ill.: InterVarsity Press, 2005).

Global Partnerships

Mary Lederleitner, *Cross-Cultural Partnerships: Navigating the Complexities of Money and Mission* (Downers Grove, Ill.: InterVarsity Press, 2010).

Brian Fikkert and Steve Corbett, *When Helping Hurts: Alleviating Poverty Without Hurting the Poor . . . and Yourself* (Wheaton, Ill.: Moody Press, 2009).

Robert Lupton, *Toxic Charity: How Churches and Charities Hurt Those They Help (and How to Reverse It)* (New York: HarperOne, 2011).

Daniel Rickett, *Building Strategic Relationships: A Practical Guide to Partnering with Non-Western Missions* (Minneapolis: STEM, 2008).

Duane Elmer, *Cross-Cultural Connections: Stepping Out and Fitting In Around the World* (Downers Grove, Ill.: InterVarsity Press, 2002).

Marvin K. Mayers and Sherwood G. Lingenfelter, *Ministering Cross-Culturally: An Incarnational Model for Personal Relationships* (Grand Rapids: Baker, 2003).

J. Mack Stiles and Leeann Stiles, *Mack & Leeann's Guide to Short-Term Missions* (Downers Grove, Ill.: InterVarsity Press, 2000).

Meic Pearse, *Why the Rest Hates the West: Understanding the Roots of Global Rage* (Downers Grove, Ill.: InterVarsity Press, 2004).

Duane Elmer, *Cross-Cultural Servanthood: Serving the World in Christlike Humility* (Downers Grove, Ill.: InterVarsity Press, 2006).

Notes

• • •

Introduction: *Missional Is Not a Word*

page 14   "To accept Christ is to enlist": James S. Stewart, *Thine Is the Kingdom: The Church's Mission in Our Time* (Edinburgh: St. Andrew's Press, 1956), p. 14.

Chapter 3: Ready Feet

page 53   "There is not a square inch": *Abraham Kuyper: A Centennial Reader*, ed. James D. Bratt (Grand Rapids: Eerdmans, 1998), p. 488.

Chapter 5: Joyful Soul

page 83   "Our lives must be connected": Mother Teresa and Angelo Devananda, *Total Surrender*, (Ann Arbor, Mich.: Servant Publications, 1985), p. 99.

Chapter 6: Purposeful Family

page 96   "And you will I'm sure ask me": *Mother Teresa*, directed by Ann and Jeanette Petrie, narrated by Richard Attenborough (New York: Petrie Productions, 1986), DVD.

Conclusion: The Missional Motivation

page 179   "In the last resort, the one reason for missions": James S. Stewart, *Thine Is the Kingdom: The Church's Mission in Our Time* (Edinburgh: St. Andrew's Press, 1956), p. 14.

LIKEWISE. *Go and do.*

A man comes across an ancient enemy, beaten and left for dead. He lifts the wounded man onto the back of a donkey and takes him to an inn to tend to the man's recovery. Jesus tells this story and instructs those who are listening to "go and do likewise."

Likewise books explore a compassionate, active faith lived out in real time. When we're skeptical about the status quo, Likewise books challenge us to create culture responsibly. When we're confused about who we are and what we're supposed to be doing, Likewise books help us listen for God's voice. When we're discouraged by the troubled world we've inherited, Likewise books encourage us to hold onto hope.

In this life we will face challenges that demand our response. Likewise books face those challenges with us so we can act on faith.

likewisebooks.com

.